BUILDING NEIGHBORHOOD ORGANIZATIONS

Building Neighborhood Organizations

A Guidebook Sponsored by the
National Association of Neighborhoods

James V. Cunningham
and Milton Kotler

University of Notre Dame Press
Notre Dame & London

Library of Congress Cataloging in Publication Data

Cunningham, James V.

    Building neighborhood organizations.

    Bibliography: p.
    Includes index.
    1. Community organizations – United States – Case
studies.   I. Kotler, Milton.   II. National Association of
Neighborhoods (U.S.)   III. Title.
HN65.C85   1983   361.8'0973   83-1182
ISBN 0-268-00668-7
ISBN 0-268-00669-5 (pbk.)

Manufactured in the United States of America

Contents

v

Figures

"The neighborhoods." Everyone talks about them, but no one in the city's power structure does anything about them. What success the neighborhoods have had toward rehabilitation is based more on local organizations than any encouragement from downtown.

—Emmett Dedmon, *Chicago*,
Vol. 32, No. 1, 1983

Preface

Neighborhood organizing in the United States has entered a new era. Gone is the novelty of the 1960s and 1970s when such organizing was a fresh adventure for most people. Gone, too, are the easy-flowing federal funds of those decades which enabled ambitious, energetic organizations to grow easily. The many organizations that survive tend to be lean, serious, and authentically rooted in their communities, while the new ones starting up are quiet, determined, and often have leaders who have been through it before. There seems now to be less shouting and more careful effort to get things done.

Neighborhood organizations have become established, important in the lives of cities, and collectively significant to the life of the nation. They give people increased control of their local turf. They deliver certain services and meet some needs better than governments, corporations, and large institutions. And they influence the policies of governments, corporations, and institutions.

As a new emphasis on localism sweeps the country, the federal government is abandoning many responsibilities and seeking to pass them to cities and states. Neighborhood organizations, as fundamental units of localism, face increased responsibilities and difficulties. Needs of neighborhood people for jobs and security increase. Opporunities to act multiply, but funds available decrease. This guidebook has been compiled to help neighborhood people and their organizations be better able to grasp opportunities. It does this by looking at the struggles of fifteen important but not always successful neighborhood organizations spread around the nation.

This guidebook is an attempt to learn from experience how to build more effective neighborhood organizations, and nothing more. It is not a definitive work on organizing. It does not answer large, theoretical questions about neighborhoods. It is intended to be a helpful how-to-do-it book rooted in reality, with a thought-provoking perspective on the future of neighborhood organizing.

The fifteen cases reveal that the new era in neighborhood organizing is but one more chapter in the historical effort of urban people to seek justice and equality.

U.S. cities originally were shaped by real estate developers, merchants, banks, transportation enterprises, manufacturers, bondholders, and media. Local governments were created to facilitate, implement, and maintain infrastructure and services essential to enterprise. The story of a Baltimore, Chicago, Wichita, or San Francisco is largely a tale of initiatives, investments, and influence by entrepreneurs, wealthy families, and corporations.

What little local challenge and competition there have been to the decisions of these economic forces have come from a loose mass of community elements, including local churches, public interest organizations, consumer co-ops and credit unions, fraternal societies, ethnic and racial groups, small community businesses and agencies, socially oriented trade unions, and neighborhood organizations. These community elements, and others like them, have long been numerous. Prior to the 1960s, however, they were fragmented, their power more potential than real.

Until the 1960s such communal forces operated through relatively few feeble organizations. Then came the "communal revolution" with the demands of women, students, minorities, consumers, environmentalists, neighborhood residents, and others for a larger voice and greater share in the power and wealth of society. This revolution spawned a host of communal organizations, with neighborhood organizations among the most significant.

Now both economic and communal forces seem indispensable to the city. Through production, jobs, and profits, economic forces provide the material resources of a city. Through family life, friendships, group worship, small institutions, and neighborhood locales, community forces provide the essential human and spiritual relationships of a city.

Resources and community are the city's twin supports. When they are in balance, as they apparently were in a few colonial cities, then the urban place is relatively happy and prosperous. When there is extreme imbalance, as in industrial cities of the late nineteenth century, the economic elements tend to overwhelm, exploit, and even destroy communal integrity.

Since World War II corporations, banks, real estate developers, downtown associations, shopping centers, large institutions such as hospitals and universities, and other major economic organizations have grown and helped cities to prosper. Generally these economic organizations have pushed rapid change and development. They have done this with their own plans and investments. And they have also done it with their influence over local government.

The role of local government in cities seems to have been much less that of initiator than that of reactor, referee, and coordinator. A few sophisticated governments seek to help achieve balance between economic and communal forces, but most of the case studies in this guidebook provide evidence that the balance is not yet near at hand. Communal forces appear still to be working uphill toward a parity of power.

Yet neighborhood organizations are now more important than they have ever been in the lives of cities. They are uniquely positioned to mobilize people to assert community interests and help achieve a balance of power with economic forces, and equal influence over local government. As will be seen, neighborhood organizations can do much to protect their own turf. Moreover, they generally possess insights into local conditions, enjoy the trust of community residents, and have accumulated skills and experience that make them appropriate vehicles for filling the service gaps caused by cutbacks in federal funds.

Neighborhood organizations have a history of supplying services. A few neighborhood organizations began contracting with local governments to provide citizen involvement in urban renewal planning back in the 1950s, and many contracted for antipoverty programs in the late 1960s, supplying child development services, job and skills training, tutorial programs, housing improvement, emergency welfare assistance, and the like. During the 1970s more neighborhood organizations, using Community Development Block Grant funds, performed such services as code monitoring, sidewalk repair, and lot clean-up. As this is written, neighborhood organizations in many cities are facing rising demands for basic life-support services such as food, medical care, emergency shelter, jobs, and legal aid. They are moving to meet these demands.

It appears that the importance of neighborhood organizations is increasing rapidly, both as community power builders and as providers of services. As these activities grow, and neighborhood organizations increase in strength, they contribute to a balance of economy and community with the accompanying increase in equality and justice such a balance promotes.

The authors have studied fifteen neighborhood organizations over a period of five years, visiting each one, interviewing the leaders periodically in person and by telephone, and examining key documents. The organizations have been observed as they have survived the 1970s and as they have attempted to utilize the opportunities of the new era begun in the 1980s.

The study has focused on the building and rebuilding of these organizations, their processes, strategies, procedures, and techniques. How each organization is put together, the way it operates, and its techniques for seeking power are given attention over issues. This is done to provide usable information for operating and building an existing neighborhood organization, or for starting an effective new one.

This guidebook begins with a chapter defining the neighborhood and setting forth its significance in our time, and a chapter defining the neighborhood organization and its way of operating.

After these first two chapters comes a summary chapter describing the steps for starting a neighborhood organization, drawn from the case studies. Then come the case studies themselves, separated into three types: (1) low-budget volunteer groups which are getting things done mainly by putting pressure on government; (2) big-budget neighborhood organizations, largely dominated by staff, heavily involved in operating services and economic development projects; and (3) neighborhood organizations closely tied to government and politics, the newest type.

After the case studies comes an analysis of what the cases seem to tell us with a cataloguing of useful ideas found in the cases. Then there is a chapter about the indispensable organizers and their secrets, and finally a few words on the future of neighborhood organizing, with a proposal for neighborhood organizations to take an expanded role in cities.

At the end will be found a list of the best books on neighborhood chosen by thirty-three people with a long-time neighborhood interest. This short list of classics is provided for those who want to deepen their understanding of neighborhoods and neighborhood organizations without drowning in the flood of literature engulfing us. There is also a detailed index to make it easy to find information on a specific topic anywhere in the guidebook.

The National Association of Neighborhoods (NAN) hopes this guidebook will prove to be a useful and important how-to-do-it reference work built, as it is, on experiences within the neighborhood movement itself. If well received and used widely, this manual will be updated and expanded periodically to maintain and increase its usefulness to neighborhood people and their organizations. Users are urged to submit ideas, suggestions, corrections, practical tips, new case studies, questions, criticisms, and the like to the National Association of Neighborhoods.

Acknowledgments

This guidebook was compiled during the volatile years 1977 through 1982. It draws on the rich experience of citizens struggling to preserve and improve their local communities in a time of economic uncertainty. It is built around fifteen original case studies of important neighborhood organizations from across the nation, describing how each has sought to build its strength. Many people have contributed by gathering facts, sharing information and opinion, and commenting on the drafts.

Assisting directly with the research have been Denys Candy, David Feehan, John Zingaro, Karon Hudock, Chi Louie, and William F. (Bob) Cunningham.

This has been a project of the National Association of Neighborhoods, and it has been given direction by a special publications committee made up of Carter Garber, Dick Cook, Ormond Harriot, Mary Seaton, Ed Schwartz, and Ron Shiffman. In addition, Roger S. Ahlbrandt, Jr., Morton Coleman, Howard Hallman, David Bergholz, Nelson Rosenbloom, Richard Rich, and Steve Glaude have given help and advice.

Busy leaders of neighborhood organizations and city agencies have spent time answering our questions and supplying their insights. These include: Sarah Gilbert, Mike Gragert, and Lois Barrett (Wichita); Mary Beth Acuff, Pat Turrieta, Bobbi Miller, Mary Lou Hayward, and Anna Muller (Albuquerque); Carlton Maynard, Jim Harrison, and Gloria Sims (Greensboro); William Hausen, James Vallas, Eleanor Bergholz, and Richard Miller (Pittsburgh); Regis Ryan, Paulette Honeygoskey, and Joy Kronenberger (McKees Rocks); Florence Bittner, David Nimkin, Beverly Peck, and L. Wayne Horrocks (Salt Lake City); Mary Pederson, Patti Jacobsen, Andy Raubeson, Jerry Mounce, Margaret Strachan, and Geri Ethen

(Portland); Bill Ariano, Larry Pencak, Joe Coffee, Phil Perkins, Ben Garber, Dick Cook, and David Biegel (Baltimore); Ben Stewart, Tip Hillan, Harriet Witt, and Wade Woods (San Francisco); Phillip Morrow, Ben Andrews, Lou Bond, and Jack Mimnaugh (Hartford); Dick Simpson, Ed Marciniak, Bruce Young, and Judy Stevens (Chicago); and Susan Meehan, Josephine Butler, Lili Iravani, and Frank Smith (Washington).

Overall quality of the book has been considerably improved by the suggestions of the editors, Ann Rice and Beth Luey.

Sound criticism and useful ideas have been supplied by our wives, Rita and Greta. We are indebted to Greta Kotler for her monumental two volumes of case studies which form a major part of the final report of the National Commission on Neighborhoods.

The essential clerical work has been done by Judy Zakaria, Mary Pat Campbell, Janet Rosenkrantz, and Linda Wykoff.

The authors are grateful to all of these able and generous people, and take full responsibility for the contents and especially for the analysis and conclusions.

Funds making this guidebook possible have come from the Office of Research of the University of Pittsburgh, the Westinghouse Electric Corporation, and the Aetna Life and Casualty Foundation.

1. What Is a Neighborhood?

Usually a neighborhood is described merely as a small territory containing people and organizations that interact. But the more we learn about the neighborhood, the more it stands out as a community of great importance.

In the life of urban people there are many communities. Each of these communities is primarily useful for different purposes. The municipal community is chiefly responsible for an orderly, convenient, and just local life. The regional community sustains a good deal of our economic activity. The work community provides a wage for our service. The neighborhood community provides most of us with shelter and opportunity for human relationships.

These purposes and communities overlap. For example, although the municipality is responsible for order and security, that responsibility is widely shared with neighborhood organizations which conduct crime watch programs and other volunteer security activity. Although the region sustains a good deal of our economic activity, it is imperative that the municipality actively plan for its economic growth; otherwise, it will stagnate. Although the downtown office pays our salary for work performed, it is not unlikely that a neighbor helped us get our job. And although the neighborhood may be the center of our social life, the quality of this life is deeply affected by corporate decisions and municipal policies. All of these communities are important to the urban dweller, for they furnish financial support, personal safety and sustenance, justice, and the essential human relationships of friendship and camaraderie.

Our chief concern in this guidebook is with the neighborhood community. As we explore this focal point of human relationships for most people, it is important not to confuse the social life of human beings with the narrow notion of entertainment. When Aristotle defined human beings as social animals, he did not mean that the pleasure of "socializing" is the essence of our humanity. He and many philosophers after him meant that human beings achieve their humanity principally through their relationships or responsibility to one another. Our God-given human dignity is maintained, not through the pursuit of pleasure, but through service to other human beings.

When we say that the neighborhood is the center of social life, we mean that for many of us our opportunities to respond to other people's needs arise largely in the daily life of neighborhood community. We are daily called upon to mourn the passing of neighbors, to console remaining kin, to support families who are separating, to guide neighboring children who seek our avuncular attention, to help repair a house, or to assist neighbors who are in financial distress. It is this continuing practice of human responsibility to others that builds both our own humanity and the social fabric of our neighborhood community.

Indeed, there are urban people who live their lives at the level of metropolis, nation, or even the world and have no attachment to the small, local community we call neighborhood. But they are a minority. In 1980 one of the authors of this guidebook participated in a survey of 5,896 households in Pittsburgh and found 63% expressed more loyalty to their neighborhood than to the city. Over half visited regularly with neighbors and performed many other of their principal life activities in and near their neighborhood.* We are confident a majority of U.S. people remain oriented to their neighborhoods. The case studies which follow give further evidence of this attachment.

The neighborhood is not the only local community that claims our responsibility to others. The workplace and municipality also make their claims. Our municipality cannot maintain order if we do not act toward one another as responsible citizens. However, it is in the neighborhood community that our responsibilities are most direct and personal.

Within the neighborhood, our responsibilities to others are sometimes exercised with and through institutions. Our responsibili-

---

* For more about the Pittsburgh survey, see Roger S. Ahlbrandt, Jr., and James V. Cunningham, *Pittsburgh Residents Assess Their Neighborhoods* (Pittsburgh: University of Pittsburgh School of Social Work, and University Center for Social and Urban Research, December, 1980).

ty to our children depends very much on the quality of our children's school, and our accessibility to that school. The school is as much a vehicle for the engagement of parental responsibility for the children of the family as it is for the exercise of public responsibility to the children of the city. The social manners and safe streets of our community are important to the equanimity and physical security of our family and friends. Our neighborhood stores help us to meet conveniently our responsibilities for the care, feeding, and shelter of our family. Our churches and synagogues help us to meet our responsibilities to God, our loving Creator. And our neighborhood organizations help stimulate a sense of responsibility where it is weak, and counteract forces irresponsible toward our common well-being.

In saying these things about human responsibility, we leave considerable room for the errors of judgment, understanding, and knowledge that are frequently made in the course of trying to exercise our responsibilities to others. There are also errors of spirit, due to fear or hardheartedness. Intelligence and good will always struggle against ignorance and narrowness to exercise human responsibility. Keeping this caution in mind, it is still true that our neighborhood institutions are only as vital as our commitment to others. The quality of our neighborhood life depends fundamentally on the vitality of our own humanity, which often is manifested in neighborhood organizations and their work.

Neighborhood is the smallest operating unit in a city above family and block club. It is the arena where a variety of human relationships develop from people living close together. As Lewis Mumford has written, "neighbors are people united primarily not by common origins or common purposes but by the proximity of their dwellings in space. . . . There is nothing forced in this relationship and to be real it need not be deep: a nod, a friendly word, a recognized face, an uttered name—this is all that is needed to establish and preserve in some fashion the sense of belonging together." But often relationships in the neighborhood go much deeper. They are intimate human relationships of kinship and friendship that can constitute a great part of our personal humanity. The neighborhood community becomes, in fact, a good part of our own human existence and induces loyalty and commitment. This is why people often fight with great passion to protect their neighborhood. The intensity of their feelings is so great that it sometimes seems irrational to outsiders. Because so much of our humanity can be rooted in our neighborhoods, residents seek power over their community affairs to better serve their responsibilities. They seek this power through community organizations, which have gained considerable power in cities throughout the country. Some neighborhood organizations govern certain affairs of their communities. This kind of self-government is a capstone to our human quest to serve others most freely.

As a community of potential intensity in our lives, a neighborhood can serve many needs and perform many functions.

A neighborhood is a market. Its households and organizations possess purchasing power with which they demand goods and services. A small part of this demand is sometimes met in the neighborhood itself, which may have shops, suppliers, and businesses of one kind and another. Since World War II, however, the tendency has been for shopping facilities to be concentrated in centralized drive-in locations outside residential neighborhoods. The neighborhood is still a market, but its purchasing power more and more flows outside the community. Market power could be important for neighborhoods to get things done, but it is seldom used by neighborhoods as leverage for neighborhood improvement. Market power can be combined in people-owned co-ops, used for boycotts, or to support neighborhood enterprise and create jobs.

The neighborhood is often an area for distribution of services. Sometimes a local distribution facility is established within the neighborhood as a school, church, employment center, clinic, senior citizen lounge, antipoverty office, or similar institution. Neighborhood organizations may deliver services to residents under contract from local, state, or federal government agencies. In these cases the citizens of the neighborhood may help shape public policy. The availability of these services and service contracts depends to a large extent on how well organized neighborhood people are to make joint demands. How well the services are used depends on the effectiveness of communication within the neighborhood, and the level of neighborhood organization.

The metropolis can be viewed as a mosaic of neighborhoods punctuated by centers of production, trade, and services or as a set of scattered commercial, industrial, cultural, and institutional centers, surrounded by interconnected and overlapping residential neighborhoods.

The neighborhood is small and relatively simple. People comprehend it. The city and region are large and complex. They are difficult to comprehend. Nearly all people feel at home in the neighborhood. It is where they can fit in as citizens.

The neighborhoods may be separated by rivers, hillsides, railroads, major streets, income level, race, nationality, and other kinds of physical and social barriers. Sometimes it is difficult for the outsider to know where one neighborhood ends and another begins. There are even situations where residents themselves are uncertain of an exact boundary.

As a piece of the metropolis, the neighborhood is volatile and dynamic. It is ever changing in small ways, sometimes in large ways. A neighborhood never stands still. It improves or declines or does some of both at the same time. If a neighborhood's improvement keeps pace with its decline, we say it is stable.

An old urban neighborhood is a product of history. It has developed over time, usually a long time – decades, centuries. It probably began as a settlement for a few people outside a small city, perhaps as the farm or estate of a single family. Buildings went up, trade grew, roads were pushed through. Stores were established. The farm or estate was subdivided into small building lots. Other settlers came to buy land and build their buildings. The settlement grew. It became a self-governing town, with schools and public offices. The city nearby crept up close. Open space disappeared. The settlement was annexed into the adjacent city. It became a neighborhood of that city but retained its identity, institutions, traditions, and personal interrelationships. Very often it kept its municipal name.

There are also tract neighborhoods, some old, some new suburban neighborhoods, that were mass built in a relatively short period, perhaps during the early 1950s or even the 1920s. Unlike earlier settlements, many of these tracts were not independent municipalities, though some had self-governing covenants. Some have been around long enough to acquire character and individuality, but many of them retain a certain military look from their uniformity and straight rows of similarly designed houses. Over time they develop functions and ways of life little different from the more randomly built neighborhoods.

The colonial cities of America were of walking scale. During the eighteenth century, craftsmen, mechanics, clerks, small shopkeepers, and their families constituted the bulk of urban society. They built small homes on the side streets, often of brick, with little gardens and some space between buildings. Around the corner, on the front streets, the rich built larger houses. Economic forces were small and did not generally overwhelm and exploit community life.

In the nineteenth century urban population expanded, with factory and mill workers becoming numerous. Jerry-built tenements were constructed close to the sprawling, bleak work places. The rich isolated themselves in choice areas. The industrial city developed with its segregation of people into neighborhood by income and occupation, and eventually by race and nationality. This became particularly marked during and after the Civil War, a period of most rapid industrial expansion. The city became like the corporation with its hierarchy and separation of classes.

Some of the immigrants and rural Americans coming to urban places settled in industrial towns adjacent to cities. Many such outlying communities were founded during the nineteenth century, populated in part by established working people moving out from the overcrowded city. During the late nineteenth and early twentieth centuries many such municipalities lost their independence as they were annexed to the central city. This tradition of municipal liberty perhaps helps to explain today's sense of neighborhood awareness in many urban neighborhoods.

For decades, governmental agencies that make and implement plans for urban improvement have recognized the neighborhood as a handy action area. Planning departments draw neighborhood plans, and urban renewal authorities designate project areas which turn out to be neighborhoods. Model cities programs were set up largely on a neighborhood or multineighborhood base.

Governments recognize neighborhoods as logical, small, bite-sized units of the metropolis where planning and renewal action can be undertaken in a manageable area. Particularly now that citizen participation has become essential to large-scale planning and renewal efforts, the neighborhood with its local organizations is utilized as the appropriate unit for development.

But government alone cannot preserve or renew a neighborhood. Thousands of individuals, families, institutions, merchants, banks, organizations, and corporations must make positive decisions to invest time, energy, and money. The quality of structures in a neighborhood is related to several factors, but there are two which dominate: economics and commitment.

Sound housing or commercial buildings cost money to buy or rent and to maintain. To keep a housing stock attractive, the people owning and occupying it need adequate income. The owners must have access to loan funds when needed and be willing to spend adequately on improvements and maintenance. Governmental code enforcement and urban renewal programs can help maintain a neighborhood's housing stock, but in the final analysis it is the financial resources of owners and occupiers and their willingness to spend that determine quality. Willingness to spend comes from loyalty and commitment to the neighborhood.

Owners and occupiers are the citizens of the neighborhood. Their interest and confidence can best be generated by organization. When neighborhood people organize to take control over their local turf, their loyalty and enthusiasm are turned inward, focused on their own up-close neighborhood needs. They get things together. Then they have power. They can pool their power with organized people in other neighborhoods and other cities to do something about economics and politics. Neighborhood organization can be a powerful process, and it is being used by millions of people in cities across the nation.

Thousands of neighborhoods from coast to coast have volunteer organizations seeking to assert some control over their turf, direct preservation and renewal. These organizations and their leaders have created and perfected strategies and techniques. This manual is an attempt to record some of these strategies and techniques to help people in troubled, unorganized, or underorganized neighborhoods who want to build powerful neighborhood organizations.

In the chapters that follow we will be concerned with what neighborhood organizations are and how effective ones get built. Through such organizations, neighborhood people can attain a new degree of freedom and power to enhance the vitality of their humanity.

2. What Is a Neighborhood Organization?

Building neighborhood organizations and using them to improve life in local communities has become an enormously important activity in the United States. There are already more than ten thousand neighborhood organizations which have stimulated a great outpouring of citizen involvement in public affairs. Neighborhood organizations now share significantly in the governance of U.S. society. Through these organizations, neighborhood people take responsibility for some of their own needs and help solve pressing problems, while at the same time strengthening the social fabric of their local communities in the face of the bewildering complexity and power of institutions, corporations, and governments.

A neighborhood organization is a group of dedicated people working to improve their local community. More formally, it is an ongoing voluntary association in a small territory, organized by residents and local businesses and institutions to act upon a variety of issues vital to the well-being of their territorial community. As will be seen in the case studies, small territorial communities (neighborhoods) can vary greatly, and neighborhood organizations come in many sizes and types, and have many different ways of doing things.

Neighborhood organizations are able to wage responsible wars of pressure and advocacy to ensure that a just share of available resources goes to neighborhoods. They can fill gaps by furnishing services and creating jobs. Neighborhood organizations can help prevent erosion of economic and social well-being in a time of retrenchment with their social action and their local enterprises.

Large, hard-to-deal-with bureaucratic organizations dominate most spheres of human life, threatening sense of community and

8

personal values. Along with family, friendship networks, and religion, the ties of neighbors and neighborhood organizations are a counterforce protecting social fabric and values. The relationships of local people are enriched and reinforced by neighborhood organizations. Beliefs in self-determination, self-reliance, family life, social justice, and the worth of every person are provided a climate in which to be freely considered and embraced.

Neighborhood organizations open new opportunities for citizens to exercise a public role. Such organizations serve as schools of citizenship and political leadership. They can heighten the sense of civic values, increase social responsibility, and democratically spread out power. Also, unfortunately, they can lead to narrowness and exclusion.

The usefulness of neighborhood organizations to city government in pointing out what services and improvements are most needed is growing. In the private market, buyers' decisions help direct production, while the public market generally has lacked this kind of useful direction. Neighborhood organizations now provide a new kind of demand articulation to help local governments make the best use of tax funds.

Generally, a neighborhood organization seeks to serve all the people of its territory and is general-purpose rather than single-issue; that is, it is ready to deal with almost any serious local need or problem that arises. Neighborhood organizations usually are started by a few concerned residents, sometimes at the urging of outside organizers. Local business people and leaders of neighborhood institutions may also be involved.

Nearly all neighborhood organizations, including the ones described in this guidebook, seek to control what happens to their home territory. They try to protect their local community and exert power over events within their neighborhood's boundaries. They attempt to influence outside organizations and agencies that can affect their neighborhood. In short, neighborhood organizations serve as vehicles through which neighborhood people take responsibility for ensuring that the rights of their neighborhood are respected and the needs of their people are met.

Neighborhood organizations gain varying amounts of control, power, and influence because they represent numbers—or at least are thought to represent numbers—and because they deploy their numbers effectively. Perhaps the active core of a neighborhood organization is only ten or twelve people in a neighborhood of eight thousand, as in the Midtown Citizens Association case. But when a serious issue arises, like an expressway to be pushed through the neighborhood, location of a new swimming pool, or the rezoning of land, the small core can usually turn out hundreds of people at a mass meeting.

Because we live in a democratic society, numbers mean power and influence. People are voters. They vote at a neighborhood polling place. Officeholders respect and fear organized citizens. Elected officeholders such as mayors, council members, magistrates, and state legislators set policy for local government and appoint some of the key officials who put public policy into effect. Because the people mobilized by neighborhood organizations are voters, these organizations are listened to by local government. Through their influence over city government, neighborhood organizations also influence corporations, institutions, private agencies, and other forces likely to affect the neighborhood. For instance, if a hospital wants to expand, it must usually obtain zoning changes from city government. If a neighborhood organization has strong influence with city government, then it can have some say over whether the zoning changes are granted. This means the neighborhood organization has some control over the hospital.

There are other ways a neighborhood organization can influence hospitals, corporations, social agencies, and the like: by persuasion and negotiation backed by careful research; by a dramatic new proposal such as transforming a block of blighted apartment houses into renovated, solar-powered, commonfolk condominiums owned by neighborhood people through sweat equity and low-interest government-aided loans; by demonstrations and publicity (or threats of these) that might harm the public image of the hospital, corporation, or agency and thereby hurt its sales or fundraising.

A neighborhood organization can help employees of an institution, corporation, or agency form a union, or support an existing union. Neighborhood organizations can also use lawsuits to stop or impede undesirable actions by others. Boycotts are another weapon. But most often the simplest, easiest, surest way for the neighborhood organization to control these institutions is by getting local government to do it. Influence over local government means influence over institutions, corporations, and social agencies.

Some neighborhood organizations, as will be seen in the Portland,

Oregon, case, have working relationships with the industry in their area which enables them to negotiate solutions to conflict at the neighborhood level. Others, such as the Shadyside Action Coalition in Pittsburgh, have institutions as integral parts of the neighborhood organization. Institutions, corporations, and social agencies are not always adversaries of neighborhood organizations. They can be working partners—sometimes.

When the people of a neighborhood, through a neighborhood organization or perhaps a set of such organizations, begin to control what is going to happen in their own neighborhood, this self-determination means their rights are being respected and their liberty enlarged. The dignity of neighborhood people is increased, their social well-being enhanced. Neighborhood people participating in public activities tend to become knowledgeable and able citizens. And they tend to strengthen relationships with their neighbors.

When a neighborhood organization persuades a company to open a needed drugstore in its area or stops an unneeded motel, initiates a day-care service, cleans up a nearby riverbank, sponsors housing rehabilitation, gets city government to improve police patrols, or otherwise provides protection or improvement, the physical well-being of the neighborhood and its people is enhanced. Of course, improvements to the physical environment affect peace of mind and social well-being, too.

When a neighborhood organization does things that protect family life, encourage friendships and neighboring, and strengthen neighborhood churches, shopping streets, and other institutions, the neighborhood organization is fostering the interrelationships of neighborhood people and strengthening social fabric and sense of community.

Tighter bonds among neighborhood people are also promoted by organized communications within the neighborhood—newsletters, neighborhood newspapers, cable TV networks, even telephone chains and community bulletin boards—all of which can be sponsored by neighborhood organizations. Communications is related to neighborhood education and training, two essential elements of neighborhood life which the cases will show are somewhat neglected.

As we get into the cases, we will see that organizations vary in the way they are put together (structure), in how they try to improve things (strategy), and in the manner in which they deal with city government, social agencies, institutions, and corporations (approach). Yet they vary within a narrow range. Only a few ways are now known for building and operating neighborhood organizations. So, for the person or group who wants to build a new organization or strengthen an existing one, there are only a small number of alternatives to be studied.

The structure, strategy, and approach of an organization will depend somewhat on the beliefs and social views of the active members who start it and run it. One of the most important beliefs that shapes an organization concerns the source of a neighborhood's problems. Do the members believe the neighborhood's problems come from weakness within neighborhood people, or from some defect in the social system? If there are blighted apartments, is their deterioration caused by sloppy and destructive tenants, or by a real estate company out to make a fast killing?

A further example would be a neighborhood organization faced with a health problem in its area: many illnesses, with people experiencing difficulty in obtaining treatment. If the organizational leadership takes an individual view, the organization might seek to educate people in how to travel on public transportation to a clinic, and furnish them with passes. Or it might set up classes to teach people how to stay healthy, and even get a doctor to come in two nights a week to treat people. These solutions seek to solve the illness problem by changing the ill people.

However, if the members of the organization take a social system view, they might try to establish a new health maintenance organization in the neighborhood, with complete health facilities, and under the control of neighborhood people. Or they might pressure a hospital to establish a health center in the neighborhood, governed by a board of residents. The members could join with other neighborhood organizations to press for national health insurance legislation. These are system solutions.

Most organizations try to help the individual. This leads to much easier solutions (or supposed solutions) than if an organization tries to change the system. Much more is known about servicing individuals than about changing systems. Also, there is the matter of resistance. A new service being set up to assist individuals may not threaten any part of society, but a change in the system can have drastic effects on a local government or some private agency, corporation, or institution.

Most neighborhood organizations eventually try to deal with both individual and social system defects, but are constantly pulled toward services which will remedy individual defects. This will be seen in several of the cases, especially in Albuquerque, Salt Lake City, McKees Rocks, Baltimore, and Hartford. But there are exceptions, such as the Shadyside Action Coalition in Pittsburgh, which has doggedly stayed away from offering services while continuing to pressure for system solutions to its neighborhood's problems.

People forming neighborhood organizations aimed primarily at social system change will often use coalition for the organization's structure, rather than individual membership. Their strategy usually will be pressure rather than service, and their approach to targets will be campaign and conflict rather than cooperation. People forming an organization aimed at curing people's weaknesses are more likely to use a membership structure, a service strategy, and a cooperative approach. But not always, as we shall see.

Neighborhood organizations are built on three different kinds of structures. Most common is the membership structure, where individuals or families join and represent only themselves. There is also the coalition structure, where the members are organizations and institutions. A third, newer kind of structure is found in organizations tied closely to government and politics. These consist of representatives of subneighborhood territories elected by their local constituencies. Combination structures are rare, but possible.

Probably the most significant difference among neighborhood organizations is that of strategy. As we look at the fifteen organizations in the cases we will see that some follow a pressure strategy, some a service strategy, and some a combination of the two which we call a mixed strategy. It is also possible to foresee other strategies.

Organizations following the pressure or advocacy strategy try to get things done indirectly by pushing someone else to do it. Usually the someone else is government, although sometimes it is a business, an individual property owner, or an institution like a hospital or university. The pressure strategy is a political way of operating and is sometimes called a social action or protest strategy.

The service strategy is direct. Instead of pressing city hall to clean up vacant lots, the neighborhood organization following a service strategy recruits teams of local volunteers who clean up the lots. The service strategy is a self-help way of doing things. The neighborhood organization following a service strategy supplies services directly to people in its area. These services might be anything from day care to low-cost groceries.

Some neighborhood organizations follow a mixed strategy combining pressure and service. Such organizations usually start out with only a pressure strategy or only a service strategy, and then over time move to using both strategies.

Other strategies are bubbling up in a few places. We have mentioned *values,* the basic beliefs of neighborhood people. Organizing has gone on in Philadelphia and elsewhere using positive common values such as security, reciprocity (people help each other), and fellowship as a base for unity and for a neighborhood "social contract" among residents, with justice as its basic anchor. This new social contract strategy is built on the premise that common values are essential to social and political well-being in the neighborhood, as in a city or nation. Edward Schwartz, of Philadelphia's Institute for the Study of Civic Values, writing in the Institute's manual *Building Community,* compares the pressure and service strategies with the social contract strategy as follows:

> Some community organizations show their strength by the number of victories they can win against the establishment. Others measure it by the number of programs they sponsor. The contract technique establishes the most compelling, but fairest, standard of all—the ability of an organization to reflect and enforce the best values of those whom it pretends to represent. . . . community emerges when people discover what they share.*

Common values can bring together the people of a neighborhood. In doing so, values help form a social fabric. Research done in several Pittsburgh neighborhoods indicates that social fabric is related to residents' commitment to their neighborhood.** If there is strong social fabric, with sharing of values and close ties among peo-

* Edward Schwartz, *Building Community* (Philadelphia: Institute for the Study of Civic Values, 1976), p. 5.

** For a report on the Pittsburgh research, see Roger S. Ahlbrandt, Jr., and James V. Cunningham, *A New Public Policy for Neighborhood Preservation* (New York: Praeger, 1979).

ple, then people are more likely to be loyal to their neighborhood, to stay in it, and to help improve it.

Common values may be the most important source of social fabric, but they are not the only source. Social fabric also flows from kinship ties, friendships, neighboring, local institutions, communications devices, and shared history. Since neighborhood organizations promote ties among people, they themselves are an important source for building social fabric. The social fabric strategy involves neighborhood people discovering and strengthening the various sources of social fabric within their neighborhood.

Other new strategies are probably being tried in neighborhoods somewhere. The final three cases in this guidebook portray organizations with direct ties to local government or party politics. These could be said to be creating a new strategy, although basically they are using a variation of the pressure strategy.

As will be seen in the cases, organizations have three legitimate ways to approach local government, a corporation, social agency, or an institution that they seek to influence. The three are cooperation, campaign, and conflict. Cooperation is a low-key, friendly approach. Campaign is a friendly but firm approach, with some pressure applied. Conflict is a militant and unfriendly approach in the face of refusal and resistance. We will see in the cases that all three approaches are useful for a neighborhood organization to master and to have ready for use when needed. An effective organization knows when to use which approach. Such skill comes mainly with experience, although study and training can help.

The case studies and commentary in this guidebook have been compiled to help readers decide whether a membership or coalition structure is better for building a new organization. They are designed to assist readers to know when to select a pressure, services, or mixed strategy. And the case studies should also help readers better know when to use a cooperative, campaign, or conflict approach.

To make full use of the cases, it is useful first to review how a neighborhood organization is formed.

3. Building a New Neighborhood Organization

Creating a neighborhood organization is a difficult undertaking but potentially has a high payoff.

A neighborhood organization may grow out of a neighborhood crisis, such as occurs when there is much visible unemployment among youth, a rash of street muggings, the threatened closing of a school, or the sudden announcement that numerous rental housing units are to be converted to condominiums. People react to such crises, and if just a few will take leadership, an organization can get started. The crisis generator might also be threatened changes in land use and city government neglect, as in the case of Wichita's Midtown Citizens Association. A neighborhood organization can be brought into being when a historic old home is to be used for unwanted commercial or institutional purposes, as in the case of Albuquerque's Downtown Neighborhoods Association.

A neighborhood organization can also arise when there is no crisis. Such organizations are catalyzed by an organizer, who might be a concerned resident or the staff member of an interested governmental or nonprofit body inside or outside the neighborhood. In the next chapter, we look at an "organizer-started" neighborhood organization in the Shadyside neighborhood of Pittsburgh. In such cases the organizer does not always have a preselected issue around which to rally residents, but seeks to build on whatever issues are bothering people.

Whether a crisis or the efforts of an organizer provoke people, the organization begins when a few of those provoked come together to talk over their concerns. They agree something has to be done. Possible actions are discussed. A start-up team or cadre emerges.

A cadre is essential for building a new organization. The cadre is simply a small group committed to trying to resolve an issue or two, and thereby to improve life in the neighborhood. Out of such effort comes the neighborhood organization. John Huenfeld, in *The Community Activists Handbook,* talks about the cadre: "Actually, three or four people who can work well together and who are prepared to follow a few systematic guidelines are far more effective than a hall full of undirected and uncoordinated human energy." (p. 4)

As the cadre moves on an issue, it recruits additional members. It grows and becomes an organization. As the original leaders of the cadre transform their loose little group into a formal organization, they make a basic decision. They choose either to make the organization one of individual members or one of representatives of other organizations and institutions in the neighborhood. They can also move to become a political structure with elected representatives from small subareas. As the members of a cadre build one of these structures they generally give close attention to their reason for being: the issues at hand, the crisis bothering them and others in their neighborhood.

It can be helpful for the cadre to prepare a short, clear, written statement of what it wants to accomplish before choosing specific issues for action. Such a statement is most useful if based on the real world, and therefore it needs to be preceded by some careful searching out of facts concerning the issues of most interest to the members of the cadre.

Dick Cook, Baltimore organizer, has suggested questions for helping the leadership cadre select the first issue (see figure 1).

Answering such questions requires the cadre to engage in an orderly process of planning. The members research the issue. As they learn more about it, they begin to see alternative courses of action. They test out the issue and alternative actions on other people around the neighborhood. Doing this, the cadre begins to recruit resources it needs such as information, more people, money, goods, and services.

In their planning, as indicated in the previous chapter, these first active members will be guided by their beliefs and social views. In particular, their plans will be shaped by whether they see issues arising out of the defects and weaknesses of neighborhood people, or from barriers and injustices embedded in the social system. For instance, if a gang of twenty unemployed, unskilled youths is an issue, the "individual defect" view might lead to job-skills training for the youths, whereas a systems view might lead to persuading local corporations to lower employment requirements and hire the youths.

For a member of the cadre to go through a careful process of creating an organization requires a sizable commitment of time. Many hours are needed to discuss, research, and choose the most potent issues for attracting new members and producing tangible gains for the neighborhood. More hours must go into planning and organizing actions. It is in this process that values come to the surface. Cadre members begin to reveal their beliefs to one another. Glue forms to hold the cadre together if there is agreement on even a few fundamental values, such as the importance of citizen participation, justice for all people, community matters being as important as economic matters, and the significance of neighbors helping neighbors.

Time is needed for strategizing and laying a course of action to follow on each selected issue. Taking action, reassessment at various

Figure 1

Ten Questions for Evaluating the Usefulness of an Issue

1. Is the issue specific? ("Crime in the neighborhood" is not specific; "two rapes on Hanover Street" is specific.)
2. Is it concrete? ("More police protection" is not; "nightly assignment of the decoy squad to Hanover Street" is concrete.)
3. Is the impact immediate? (Is it a real thorn in the side of a lot of people? Will it make a difference to people if the issue is resolved?)
4. Is winning the issue within the organization's capability?
5. Will winning give the members a sense of their own power?
6. Will winning change the situation so that members are in fact more powerful?
7. Does the organization have sufficient resources to take on the issue? (Or can it get them?)
8. Is the target which is to be approached located in a single place? (Will it be clear to the public who the target is?)
9. Is there a basic principle involved?
10. Is the issue important to the membership? (Will it draw new members?)

stages, and continual revision of plans take more hours. When time is set aside periodically to evaluate progress and lack of progress, and to think out the consequences of possible switches in tactics, the effort becomes a training process for cadre members. They learn the hard reality of politics: that the strong win, the weak lose, and that the intrinsic value of a position sometimes means little. They find that carefully planned and executed tactics make it easier to win.

Members of the cadre consider the arena within which an issue is to be met. It might be in the neighborhood, in city hall, in the executive offices of a bank, or in county government. It might even be in the state capitol. The members of the cadre analyze the relevant power structure. Who can make the decisions to resolve the issue? How can those powerful people be reached? The cadre assesses its own position. Who is the power structure in the neighborhood? How can some of the neighborhood power elements be enlisted in the campaign to help win the issue? What about possible allies outside the neighborhood?

When a diligent cadre plans what action it will take on an issue, it schemes not only to act from strength, but also to have alternatives should one course of action suddenly be stymied. Alternatives thought out in advance give the group flexibility, keep it from becoming bogged down if there is unexpected stonewalling by the target. If the prime plan is built around expectations that the mayor will show up to bargain as invited, one alternative plan should be a course of action to follow if the mayor does not show up.

As the fledgling organization takes actions, attracts new people, wins a few small victories, writes down its objectives, adopts by-laws, and elects officers, it pushes ahead to new issues and evolves an overall strategy. If it is mainly concerned with the immediate needs of its neighborhood's people, it is likely to evolve a services strategy and set up its own service programs, as the Focus on Renewal Neighborhood Corporation has done. Or, it could adopt a pressure strategy to get government, business, and agencies to furnish services, as the Downtown Neighborhoods Association did when securing a Neighborhood Housing Services project. If the new organization is concerned principally with system change, it will most likely adopt a pressure strategy, although system change can come through a services strategy when new kinds of service institutions, housing, and economic development projects are invented and put under community control.

Most neighborhood organizations, as in the case studies, begin with a pressure strategy, but over time gravitate toward a few services or community development projects, and thereby shift to a mixed strategy. Probably the outstanding case study in this manual illustrating a mixed strategy is Southeast Community Organization. Such organizations never quite give up the use of pressure, however.

There are also organizations which start with pressure, and then drop it in favor of services and economic development, as did the Upper Albany Community Organization in Hartford.

The three political cases in Chicago, Pittsburgh, and Washington heavily involve pressure strategies, but even the organizations there have found services—such as sponsoring a neighborhood fair, publishing a voters' guide, and making referrals—creeping into their programs.

Regardless of strategy, it is important that an organization's early efforts result in a few successes, even if they are minor ones. This means careful selection of the service to be offered or the target to be pressured. Some early success is vital to encourage the new cadre, and help it expand. The people of its neighborhood need to see something happen if they are going to respond to recruitment efforts.

New neighborhood organizations following a service strategy usually have the visibility of their service to win the confidence of their fellow residents. Organizations pursuing a pressure strategy have to depend on the tangible victories which result when governments, corporations, or other organizations respond to the pressure tactics, and the publicity attendant upon such response. The organization with a pressure strategy has much less control over the elements essential to its development. It is launched on a riskier course, but a course often laced with conflict and great opportunity which participants find exciting, even though they do not win every battle.

The strategy chosen will help shape the new organization's recruiting efforts. An organization using a pressure strategy will find it easier to gain recruits among more militant residents, and especially those who are suspicious about the activities and intentions of established pillars of society such as governments, large corporations, universities, and even labor unions. More conservative residents, those with some trust in established organizations and institutions, tend to be more susceptible to the recruiting of service-oriented neighborhood organizations. Gaining a recruit for either kind of neighborhood organization, however, requires that the program of the organization somehow appeal to the interests of the people being recruited.

Early in its life, the new organization is also going to be finding its most effective and comfortable approach to other organizations and institutions from which it might seek something. As indicated in the previous chapter, an organization has three choices: it can approach the target organization in a friendly and cooperative manner, it can campaign hard to win agreement, or it can confront the target with militant demands. As will be seen in the cases, most organizations, over time, move toward a pragmatic "bag of tools" way of operating, choosing an approach to match each issue. We will see this particularly in Baltimore, where Southeast Community Organization uses cooperation, campaign, and confrontation approaches, depending on who has to be convinced about what.

In choosing which approach to use with a request or demand, the cadre tries to estimate what the response will be. Is the target likely to be agreeable, difficult, or downright defiant? Logically, an agreeable target is approached with cooperation; a difficult target, through campaign; and a defiant target, with militancy.

A neighborhood organization early learns that no approach is effective without some strength behind it. As the authors once heard in an Asian-American neighborhood: "truth and goodness triumph when the third trio member is power." Power is the capacity to achieve objectives. It is the ability of one organization to exert some control over another. If the cadre of a newly emerging organization decides it wants a recalcitrant city government to remove packs of stray dogs from its neighborhood's streets, the new organization must muster sufficient support, by way of forceful negotiation sessions with city officials, crowds at public hearings, media attention, and the like, to get city government to act. A mere request generally does not move an uncooperative government, until that government feels the request is backed by a number of voters who collectively constitute strength.

As it wins victories, the new organization is going to want to make certain that news about the victories is communicated widely. This is important to notify other possible targets of the new organization's power, and to attract money and neighborhood recruits to the organization. A little attention to communications goes a long way.

It means that a brief written statement of the new organization's position, with all essential facts, is sent to newspapers and to radio and TV stations. If possible, the organization may publish a newsletter (in time it may become a neighborhood newspaper) through which it can describe itself and its victories to many people in the neighborhood. The newsletter may set out bait for attracting new members. It may also attack enemies and pat friends on the back.

Training is a worthwhile early activity for volunteers. Research skills are especially useful to help prepare issues. Research skills can be exercised by almost any willing neighborhood volunteer who gets a little training. In any city there are colleges, civic agencies, and planning departments. These can often be called on to provide training, to aid with difficult research problems, and in some cases even to carry out complex studies which will assist neighborhood organizations. One additional benefit from research is that it helps reveal other organizations which have an interest in an issue, and therefore identifies possible allies who might join the effort to resolve the issue.

As a new organization emerges and the members of its initiating cadre gain experience, the possible benefits from formal training for the cadre members will increase. The new organization can establish its own training program simply by obtaining the services of a competent trainer or training organization. Through training, members can gain skills for recruiting, leadership development, communications and publicity, and fundraising. They can find out how to tap local and national resources. They can come to understand complex issues such as redlining and youth employment.

The trainer might be an experienced individual working as a freelance consultant, a faculty member of a university, a staff member of a citywide organization, or even a field operator from one of several national training organizations. Sometimes there will be no charge for such services, but more often there will be a fee, and if a national training organization is doing the training, the fee may be stiff. Of course, when a neighborhood organization pays for its training it can have more control and is more likely to get exactly the services it wants.

Through training, volunteer officers and members learn how to uncover the names of property owners in the county recorder's office, how to get access to police records, how to plan an agenda, how to work with the news media, how to organize a mass meeting, and how to strategize effectively. In time, some members of the cadre themselves may become capable of training new recruits.

Obtaining recruits is not a mysterious enterprise. It comes from enthusiastic members making a personal appeal to people who may benefit from winning an issue, or perhaps have a talent they want to practice. The most effective method is simply one person asking another to join the action.

People join neighborhood organizations for many reasons: Because they are angry about something. Because they want something done. Because they love their neighborhood and want to preserve it. Because they are in politics and seeking votes or in business and seeking customers. Because they are impressed with what the organization is doing. Because the organization has status. Because a friend asks them to join. Because the organization is getting a lot of publicity. Because they want some control over public decisions. Because they see a desperate need for jobs. Because they want to meet people. And so on.

All of these reasons boil down to one basic reason: benefits expected. Every human being has needs. It may be a straightforward need to protect property values threatened by a zoning change, or a wish to get the street out in front paved, or to help aged parents who need some nearby health services. It may be to advance a cause strongly felt. It may be something more personal like a chance for recognition, for making friends, or for satisfying a healthy urge to help others. People join organizations because they expect a benefit. And that's not a bad thing. Getting benefits flowing is what organizations are all about. In the beginning it is essential that cadre members find an issue they agree is important. An achievable benefit before their eyes is essential if they are to persevere.

As a new organization gains members it outgrows the simple cadre form. Distributing responsibilities among committees or task forces becomes necessary. Such dividing up works best when the committees are kept small, with each limited to people with a demonstrated interest in the committee's particular responsibility. The chief officer of the organization keeps in close contact with committee heads to encourage action, ensure internal communication, provide support, and needle as required. The fewer committees, the better. They should only be created as need forces their formation.

Money will become indispensable to the new organization. A treasury, even a small one, will increase the confidence of members that the organization is going to succeed. Members of the launching cadre probably will obtain their first funds from their own pockets. This is healthy. It firms up their commitment a bit.

The Albuquerque and Wichita case studies which follow describe organizations that have accomplished much with few dollars. The same will be seen with San Francisco's Western Addition Neighborhood Association.

As an organization expands it will tap a widening circle of neighborhood people for cash. Most contributions will likely come from those with an interest in a given issue. If an organization is going to deal with a zoning issue, it should ask money from property owners who stand to benefit. Perhaps a lawyer must be retained, photographs taken, flyers printed, buses hired to carry people to hearings. If potential beneficiaries of victory are asked to give fifty dollars toward legal fees, they are more likely to respond than if asked merely to donate to the organization.

As the organization grows and expands its field of interest, the temptation will arise to seek grants from government and foundations. There are various opinions on the wisdom of this. They shake down to two basic positions. The pro position is that an organization can do much more to meet its objectives with adequate financing; foundations and governments are the two best sources; take it if you can get it. The con position is that an organization loses some of its freedom to maneuver when it accepts such grants; the flow of cash is always for a limited period; and when the grants terminate the organization tends to suffer shock and paralysis. This situation will be seen in the Western Addition Project Area Committee. It is also argued that grants make an organization "controversy-shy," overly cautious, afraid it might offend a funding source — although this doesn't always happen, as we shall see.

There is no easy resolution to these clashing opinions. It depends somewhat upon an organization's objectives. If it wants staff and size, and the capacity to offer services, it probably makes sense to go for grants. If it aims at a lean, tough, largely pressure posture, it will resist the grant temptation and raise funds from its own local sources. The case studies will tell us more about this question.

As an organization establishes itself in its neighborhood, and searches for ways to increase its clout with government and other established institutions, it begins to consider alliances with other neighborhoods. These can be ad hoc arrangements, lasting only for the time needed to resolve a single issue. In such cases an organization of one neighborhood finds organizations in other neighborhoods with an interest in the same problem. A joint effort ensues without any permanent ties being established.

Sometimes a neighborhood finds that organizations in contiguous neighborhoods face some similar localized, long-term concerns, such as truck traffic, factory-fed air pollution, an inferior high school. Then at least a semipermanent coalition may be called for. Beyond this is the citywide, or even metropolis-wide, coalition of neighborhood organizations. There are some statewide coalitions and several national coalitions, including one which initiated this manual. Should your organization join a coalition?

Again, there are two sides. One view is that it is too expensive in time, energy, and other scarce resources to belong to a permanent coalition. Besides, it can cramp your style because you have to be careful not to take actions or make statements that might offend your coalition mates. The opposing view is the old notion of strength through unity: city hall must pay attention to a multiheaded coalition, whereas it tends to ignore small, individual organizations. Some experienced organizers now feel the outside forces with which most neighborhood groups must deal are so powerful that coalition is absolutely necessary. Such organizers feel that neighborhood groups cannot attract people and money without tackling serious economic and social issues, and that such issues call for coalition.

One final matter of importance is evaluation. This is a process, maybe best called a habit, which keeps organizations from getting smug, ensures that they learn from their experiences (and especially from their mistakes), and helps to discover new ideas and identify new issues. To benefit from evaluation, an organization builds it into its normal processes. As a cadre gets rolling it may hold important meetings with other neighborhood people, with government officials, and with other outsiders. As it plans and undertakes actions, each important step can be followed by an evaluation session among the cadre members. What went right? What went wrong? Why? What should have been done that wasn't done? Out of frank, systematic self-appraisal comes cadre development. Tough, successful organizations spring from such stuff.

The main point of this chapter is that building and operating a neighborhood organization calls for the use of many skills. The case studies that follow will describe essential skills as they are being utilized in a variety of neighborhoods. Figure 2 summarizes the organizing steps set forth in this chapter.

Figure 2

Fourteen Steps for Building
a New Neighborhood Organization

1. A crisis or an organizer's initiative provokes a few people.
2. This determined handful forms the beginning cadre.
3. The cadre defines the exact nature of the issue to be worked on and begins to move.
4. Additional members are recruited as efforts on the issue pick up steam.
5. The cadre and followers achieve some success on the issue and seek outside allies if needed.
6. The cadre and others involved move to form a permanent organization, choosing to build the structure from either existing organizations or individual members.
7. The new organization evolves a strategy: it will get things done by pressure on government and other targets, or it will provide services to people, or even try to do both.
8. The new organization picks an additional issue or two, building power, utilizing cooperation, campaigning, and confrontation as appropriate.
9. Members are trained to be more effective.
10. Regular communication is established with members and with the public.
11. A stable source of income is developed, but no more than needed.
12. Alliances are made with other organizations as useful.
13. Evaluation is made a habit.
14. Recruiting new members and facing new issues go on continuously.

4. Case Studies I:
Low-Budget, High-Pressure
Volunteer Groups

As the last chapter points out, neighborhood organizations usually start small. They are provoked into being by a need to confront a government, a corporation, or a large institution over a vital issue that arouses several neighborhood people to take action.

A majority of neighborhood organizations never move beyond this stage. Their active people remain mostly volunteers, they do not need much money, and they get most things done by pressure although they are frequently tempted to set up services. And they often go on for years doing quite well as low-budget organizations with no staff or a small staff, free from the ups and downs of government grants. Small organizations of this kind are examined in this first set of case studies.

Midtown Citizens Association (Wichita)

We start with the small Midtown Citizens Association of Wichita, Kansas, which has held to a pressure strategy for ten years and has achieved most of its goals.

Wichita sits on the edge of the Midwest, not far from Oklahoma, benefiting from urban and rural prosperity. Surrounded by rolling wheat fields, beef and dairy farms, and gas and oil wells, it is the world center for the manufacture of light airplanes, an industry hit hard by the recession of the early 1980s. First settled as a trading post in 1864, Wichita grew slowly but steadily until it became today's metropolis of one-half million people. In recent decades its

27

historic "Cowtown" trading post has been restored, and the nearby downtown has been renewed and modernized.

North of downtown, a short walk past the modern city hall, between the Little Arkansas River and the I-135 Expressway, is a two-square-mile neighborhood of neat frame houses that dates back to the 1880s. This is Midtown, the first neighborhood in the city whose residents got together to preserve their neighborhood's history and integrity.

Midtown is Midwest flat, its streets laid out in gridiron blocks, with squat trees growing along the curbs. Single-story white houses dominate, with an occasional two- or three-story Victorian home, restored and handsome. Here and there is a corner store or beer bar. In one corner of the neighborhood, garden apartments and townhouses have been built on cleared land. Commercial Broadway Street runs through the center of Midtown, lined with restaurants, motels, and shops.

Near the expressway are a few old industrial buildings and growing St. Francis Hospital. Along the river are well cared for parks and playgrounds. Although downtown's twenty-six-story Holiday Inn is visible from the neighborhood, it largely has a relaxed, small-town feel. Residents' incomes vary from welfare to middle, and there are blacks and Hispanics in a population that is predominantly white.

Back in 1972 a few residents of this idyllic little neighborhood became concerned about the declining condition of houses, obsolete industrial buildings, and what they felt was neglect by city government. City officials then seemed resigned to letting the area drift toward deterioration, demolition, and redevelopment for commercial, industrial, and institutional uses.

Most of those who began to meet, study, and plan were white-collar workers and professionals. They decided to try zoning as the tool for protecting and upgrading their attractive, but sliding, neighborhood. They were also concerned about promoting a stronger sense of community. In 1972 the neighborhood did not have a formal, recognized name. After some thought and discussion the group chose "Midtown," and within a few years the name took hold among many of the neighborhood's eight thousand people and downtown officials, with real estate companies beginning to use the name in ads.

Residents came together to form the Midtown Citizens Association, which won immediate credibility by becoming incorporated and obtaining tax-exempt and tax-deductible status from the Internal Revenue Service. Meanwhile, the association launched a fight to have the zoning of an important corner changed from commercial to residential. Staff of the city planning commission had recommended the change, but it faced opposition from planning commission members and a doubtful reception from the city commission, the city's principal governing body. The leadership cadre of this fledgling association organized letter-writing campaigns and turned out crowds for public hearings to support the staff position, and it won approval.

The city commission's favorable decision was challenged in the courts and went finally to the Kansas Supreme Court, which upheld the commission and neighborhood, establishing the important precedent that city officials can change zoning on land from a less restricted use such as commercial to a more restricted use such as residential without the permission of the owners of the land.

Made confident by its zoning victory, the small cadre of leaders mobilized residents to stop a proposed expressway inner loop which threatened to gobble up land and split off part of the neighborhood. More than three hundred residents came out to protest the loop at a hearing by the city commission. Opposition and arguments by Midtowners and others in the city were potent enough to kill the loop. Since then the residential character of the neighborhood has seemed secure.

Leaders of the association have become conscious of the need for power to achieve their goals. One goal has been to get heavy trucks off neighborhood streets. In 1975, careful research by its traffic committee convinced the association that truckers were going out of their way to use the neighborhood's one-way residential streets, and that existing state highways in and around the area could handle the truck flow. A proposal was drawn to ban truck traffic from several residential streets.

The association launched a large-scale petition campaign. It lined up support from the planning director and director of economic development, and from other citizens' groups. When the request was turned down by the traffic commission, it was appealed to the city commission which in 1976 agreed to ban truck traffic on all but one of the suggested streets. Association President Mike Gragert recognized the success of the pressure strategy, which was aimed at getting city government to accept the residents' view of what the neighborhood should be: "Behind such triumphs is an enlightened and committed city commission which, from the time the association conceived its dream for a rejuvenated Midtown, adopted that dream as its own and has since fostered and nurtured that vision so that it is now becoming reality."*

Since then the association has guided the city's planners in location of a park swimming pool and in the taking of property for urban renewal projects within the neighborhood. Such property is limited to industrial land and tenant-occupied properties which have become dilapidated. The latter effort has resulted in only a small amount of displacement of occupants.

The Midtown Citizens Association has become well established. It has a leadership cadre of twelve persons; five officers and the chairpeople of the various committees. The twelve form the executive committee, which meets monthly and gives direction to the organization. Most positions and projects originate in the executive committee but are taken to the monthly, open general membership meeting where final decisions are made. From twenty to seventy-five people attend these general meetings (the organization has a card file of four hundred people who have shown interest). Anyone who lives in the area, owns property, or has a business in the neighborhood is considered a member and may vote at general meetings including the annual election meeting. An attempt is made to publicize meetings through a mimeographed newsletter delivered to all homes and businesses in the neighborhood, and through a "telephone tree" which does not always work effectively. Association monthly meetings are held in a church basement, with babysitting provided in the church nursery. Occasionally an open potluck supper with entertainment precedes the business meeting, and helps to draw people and build personal relationships.

Although the association has emphasized pressure for getting things done, it did initiate the Midtown Construction Company to make available at least one reliable renovation contractor, willing and able to do large and small housing rehabilitation jobs. Beginning as an arm of the association, it became in time a separate nonprofit company and eventually was transformed into a profit-making business owned and operated by the general contractor who had run the

* This quote and similar quotes below are from interviews conducted by the authors, unless otherwise identified.

service from the beginning. Experience taught that a profit-making status for the company would make it easier to obtain credit from commercial lenders and get help from the Small Business Administration. The principal owner phased out the company in 1982 to do voluntary service for his church. The Mennonite Housing and Rehabilitation Service, a spinoff of Midtown Construction, is carrying on, particularly providing low-cost housing repairs for disadvantaged citizens.

Sometime after Midtown was organized and helped to stimulate voluntary neighborhood organizations in various parts of the city, city government divided Wichita into fifteen "neighborhood areas," with an elected nine-person council in each. The councils meet regularly, listen to citizens, and formulate recommendations to the commissioners who run city government. Leaders of the Midtown Association have been elected to the official council for their area, and have given direction to its program, using it as an additional channel to city hall.

The association has prospered as a purely voluntary organization. In 1979 executive committee members began to discuss raising funds for a staff person, with discussions centering around a possible grant or general fundraising drive. They did not consider asking city government for funds. Up to then the association had been getting along well on less than $2,000 a year raised by contributions, garage sales, and advertising in the newsletter. No dues were charged. The association applied for a HUD grant in 1980, but the request was turned down. Since then the association has continued to operate as a volunteer organization without staff.

Besides being the principal mechanism for communication, the newsletter (called *The Midtowner*) has been both the single largest expense and source of income. Four thousand copies of the mimeographed publication are produced six times a year on the mimeograph machine lent by St. Paul's United Methodist Church. Volunteers distribute copies to all households in the neighborhood. An average issue contains six pages of information about zoning, city plans for the neighborhood, historic preservation, yard-of-the-month awards, new shops opened, meetings and hearings held or to be held, schedules of services at neighborhood churches, and several advertisements. Ads in the newsletter remain the prime source of income of the association.

Failure to obtain a HUD grant may have been a boon to the organization. A grant would have meant staff and expansion, and then a probable loss of grant and retrenchment under the cutback policy of President Reagan.

Although without staff, the association keeps things moving. There is no formal training for its officers or members, but a few informal new member orientation programs have been held in members' homes. Some leaders take part in training offered by the city for the official neighborhood councils. This training teaches participants how to do research on their own neighborhoods, and how councils can initiate projects to utilize Community Development Block Grant funds.

As part of its neighborly services, the association has organized a work party to repair the dilapidated home of a poor senior citizen and mobilized people to bring meals to an ill elderly couple. The association has promoted social fabric through street parties, neighborhood celebrations, Halloween parties for children, and a youth football team.

The historic committee has done some research on old structures, using city records and newspapers. Beyond this, the association has made small use of research. It is noteworthy, however, for having a tradition of systematic evaluation. Each year, at a regular meeting of the executive committee, officers and committee chairpeople stop to reflect on where they have been and where they should be going, raising such questions as: What are we missing? What problems are being ignored? What new projects should we be thinking about? This process has served the association well and kept it moving ahead to new programs.

Primarily concerned with preserving housing and resisting expansion of nonhousing uses like manufacturing and heavy commerce, the association has been willing to make deals with some business firms on zoning, agreeing not to oppose some projects in exchange for certain restrictions on construction, and a veto over design. Mike Gragert is a lawyer and voluntarily assists in such arrangements.

Issues ahead include more zoning questions, which may be tougher to win in the future since new city commission members in office in the 1980s lean more toward a "progress through real estate development" viewpoint. It is expected the new members will be less supportive of historic and low-density housing than past commissions. Promoters of apartment buildings, condominiums, and shopping centers hope to find a more attentive ear in the new commission when and if the recession of 1981-82 lifts. The new commission, while not so friendly, is still cooperating with neighborhood organizations, although it is a little more cautious about restricting commercial and industrial zoning. Association members say, "It ain't as bad as we feared." However, federal cutbacks are reducing funds available for neighborhood improvements and housing loans.

The association remains alert to keeping the hospital in bounds, promoting more rehabilitation of housing, enforcing a new ordinance limiting front yard parking, and controlling the use of houses in which people are operating businesses (beauty parlors, guitar lessons, and so forth).

Midtown Citizens Association began as a pressure group, and that remains its basic thrust. However, as so many organizations do over time, it has found needs and opportunities in the neighborhood that no one else was ready to handle, so it started a remodeling contracting service and a widely circulated newsletter, and helped promote a youth football program. It also has sponsored social events and teams of volunteers to help neighbors in need. Clearly, its pressure strategy has been modified a bit.

In 1982 the association was celebrating its tenth anniversary and Mike Gragert was saying: "The association may not go on indefinitely. With success comes complacency. We don't have the same old motivation, we're more relaxed now. But somehow we continue to [attract] and produce new leaders. Maybe the shortage of housing loan funds will cause new problems we must tackle."

Midtown Citizens Association is the kind of effective, low-budget organization that could be started in almost any neighborhood where twelve people are willing to do some work. Money is not a prime concern in such an organization. Funding cuts do not destroy it.

Arlington Park Neighborhood Organization (Greensboro)

The low-budget organization in Wichita just looked at is strictly local in its organizing ties, and firm but mild in its dealings with government and others from whom it might request assistance for its neighborhood. Now we look at an organization with national ties that has been militant in its approach.

This group comes out of the ACORN school of organizing.

ACORN stands for Association of Community Organizations for Reform Now, a national network of neighborhood groups that began in Arkansas in 1972. Across the nation in the 1980s, it has been gaining considerable attention for its squatter campaign, which puts homeless people into empty houses.

The ACORN philosophy is that people's lives largely are shaped by the actions and decisions of corporations and governments far removed from the neighborhood. However, the neighborhood is where ordinary people can most readily organize and generate power. ACORN's theory is that by massing power in city, state, and national coalitions of ACORN neighborhood groups, ordinary people can achieve some control over actions and decisions of corporations and governments. ACORN has been building steadily on this philosophy and now has affiliated coalitions in twenty-seven states with a total claimed membership of 45,000. ACORN, at its annual national conventions, takes radical populist positions, supporting government ownership of utilities, wage and price controls, and more grassroots power in the Democratic party. It concentrates its organizing on low- and moderate-income neighborhoods, and each neighborhood group follows the same basic organizing process.

In North Carolina, the state affiliate is Carolina Action, which was started in Durham in 1972 by neighborhood people who wanted to fight rate increases by the Duke Power Company. They later turned to maintaining and improving their neighborhoods, and opposing downtown renewal which they feared would disrupt inner-city poor neighborhoods and absorb most of the city's resources.

This organizing effort spread from Durham to other North Carolina cities, including Greensboro. Greensboro is one of several medium-sized, modern cities in the state's Piedmont region. Greensboro textile mills pour out vast quantities of blue jeans and other fabric products. Colleges and insurance companies employ thousands. Greensboro is a city with hustle, attractive suburbs, and a renewed downtown that dies on weekends. The city has grown rapidly since 1950, with a population now estimated at 160,000. It is part of a metropolitan area of 700,000 encompassing Winston-Salem and High Point. The area is famous for furniture as well as textiles. It has survived Reagonomics with less unemployment than most northern cities.

Planning, Community Development Block Grants, and capital improvements have been used liberally in Greensboro in attempts to revitalize old neighborhoods. A small neighborhood touched by this strong action is Arlington Park, which lies south of downtown between Eugene and Asheboro streets. Arlington Park is made up of low- and moderate-income black families living in small frame and brick houses on irregular streets. It is not a crowded area. The little one-story houses have yards, there are open spaces with weeds and scrubby trees, and it boasts a nice new recreation park that gives the neighborhood its name. Arlington Park has about four hundred families living in its small houses. Most are homeowners, but a few are renters living in ramshackle duplexes. Many families subsist on Social Security or low-paying mill or service jobs.

The area has had problems. Street lights, sweeping, garbage pick-up, sidewalks, and police patrols were needs inadequately met until the residents got together in the Arlington Park Neighborhood Organization and began to push.

The Arlington Park Neighborhood Organization came into being in 1978 with organizing aid from Carolina Action/ACORN. Carolina Action has a small office and staff of organizers in Greensboro and assists residents of neighborhoods who are willing to give time and effort to forming an organization. The organization began ACORN-style with a young Carolina Action organizer going door to door, talking to residents, finding those concerned and angry about neglect of the neighborhood and inviting them to join Carolina Action at $15 per year. Eventually, she brought together a roomful of unhappy folk to discuss the bad state of their neighborhood and decide what to do. She found them tough and ready to form a cadre whose members would call their neighbors into open meetings to choose issues and plan actions.

First needs given attention were street lights and the park. With the help of the organizer, cadre members applied heavy pressure to city officials, brought them out to face indignant residents at neighborhood meetings, and mobilized large numbers at stormy city council hearings. Response came quickly. Street lights were installed and the new park developed. The organization then went on to solve other problems.

Monthly meetings regularly brought out seventy-five to a hundred residents. All who live in the neighborhood were considered members. No dues were charged by Arlington Park Neighborhood

Organization, but active members were urged to join Carolina Action/ACORN, with the $15 annual dues payable in installments on any reasonable schedule. Dues paid to Carolina Action help finance the organizer's subsistence salary and free residents from concern about money-raising, staff help, and record-keeping.

Monthly meetings have always been informal. All decisions have been made at these meetings with any resident able to speak and vote. The organization has had no permanent officers, and a different active member chairs each meeting. The Carolina Action organizer pulls together the agenda each month based on decisions and discussion at the previous meeting, and suggestions from active members. Lack of officers has conferred more than usual control on the staff, a circumstance which has helped lead to trouble.

The philosophy of the Arlington Park Neighborhood Organization, as expressed by Carlton Maynard, one of its founding members, has been: "There are laws to help us. We have to put them to work." Maynard and his fellow residents from the beginning used an aggressive pressure strategy as they sought to put the laws to work.

Carolina Action has continuously assigned one or two organizers to Greensboro, usually young college graduates paid about $400 a month. This VISTA-level salary is the standard pay for all of the dedicated, young full-time organizers who are the engine of ACORN and its affiliates such as Carolina Action. Consideration is being given to hiring part-time senior citizens who will assist the organizing efforts for a token salary.

At least four cities in North Carolina have an organizer or two at work. In addition to servicing affiliated neighborhood organizations, they also arrange discount programs for members (10 percent off on drugs, cleaning, cameras, and so on at cooperating stores). Such discounts can be an important direct benefit for members and an incentive for joining.

From some of its offices, Carolina Action operates a door-to-door fundraising program in high-income areas. Canvassers ask for contributions to help Carolina Action wage campaigns against high utility rates, for controls over trucks carrying nuclear waste through residential streets, and against a proposed site for toxic waste disposal. The highly trained young canvassers receive a percentage of money collected. Active Carolina Action members in Greensboro meet with the canvassers to ensure they understand well what the organization is doing and thinking, and also to help members keep up to date on canvassing activities. As they go door to door, the canvassers often ask residents to sign a petition on a specific issue.

In Greensboro, seven neighborhood organizations are affiliated with Carolina Action. Two elected representatives from each neighborhood sit on a city Carolina Action board, together with several at-large members representing interest in specific issues such as housing, unemployment, utility rates, and car insurance rates. This board directs the organizers and decides on certain issues for focus.

Half the members of the official Community Development Committee advising city government on allocation of federal community development funds have been Carolina Action members. They push to ensure that a fair share of funds goes to neighborhood improvements.

A Carolina Action statewide board has two representatives from each neighborhood organization in North Carolina, plus some at-large issue members. Each city board may nominate people for offices of the state organization. In 1982 there were four city boards in North Carolina, with contact work under way in other cities. In that same year, Jim Harrison, long active in Carolina Action in Greensboro, was elected a national vice-president of ACORN.

Carolina Action and ACORN acknowledge the importance of strengthening neighborhood communities but see neighborhood actions and services as tools to achieve social bonds so people can struggle cohesively in the wider political and economic arenas.

The affiliated neighborhood groups in Greensboro sent delegates to ACORN's 1980 national convention in New York, held at the same time as the Democratic National Convention. The 1,800 ACORN delegates marched, negotiated, and won agreement that the Democratic National Committee would set up a commission to seek ways to guarantee that more low- and moderate-income people would be delegates at future national party conventions, a hope that never came to fruition since in 1981-82 the party adopted policies and practices largely restoring control of conventions to elected party and public officials.

Carolina Action and ACORN believe strongly that the basic issue confronting their members is the distribution of power. Says an ACORN declaration: "We organize neighborhood groups to build a base of constituents which can wield power in its own right. It is the wielding of this power which will ultimately bring about the change."* Their national network is growing. It is becoming largely self-financing and so is little affected by the cutbacks of the Reagan era. "Unions financed their massive organizing drives out of membership dues and ACORN's goal is to do the same," is a statement often made by ACORN organizers. Such an achievement will give ACORN and its affiliates like Carolina Action considerable independence, and the freedom to take radical stands. They have already given many mayors anxious moments, and they may eventually do the same to governors and presidents. But in the meantime the ACORN national structure and militant approach sometimes lead to difficulty at the neighborhood level.

Arlington Park is an example of this difficulty. In 1980 city government was ready to respond to the neighborhood with a planned community development program. It needed a neighborhood group to work with but was turned off by the militant action, "outside organizers," and national aims of the Arlington Park Neighborhood Organization. City government wanted an independent entity that was representative of the neighborhood and not exclusive because it charged dues of any kind.

Many residents, including Carlton Maynard, did not want to lose the improvements possible through the city program. They formed the Arlington Park Neighborhood Association and obtained an incorporation charter from the state. It is an organization of volunteers with no dues, but it does have officers and meets monthly. Said Maynard about the new organization in 1982, "It's more for the people, and works more on neighborhood things without getting into statewide issues which take too much time away from the neighborhood."

Carolina Action leaders like Jim Harrison feel both groups have a role to play, with the new association able to obtain costly improvements through cooperation with the city while the old organization joins with other Carolina Action groups in Greensboro to press for such reforms as black representation on the all-white city

* Wade Rathke, Seth Borgos, and Gary Delgado, "ACORN: Taking Advantage of the Fiscal Crisis", *Social Policy,* September/October 1979, p. 35.

council. These leaders do fear that groups like the new association become too dependent on city officials.

City officials believe it is essential to have a representative and open group to work with. They find the Carolina Action staff increasingly antagonistic and feel staff members keep neighborhood groups dependent and push them into conflicts the members of the groups would rather avoid.

The tension in Greensboro is not unusual for a city where ACORN-affiliated neighborhood organizations are active. National ACORN leadership feels such tension is inevitable if community people are to build true power.

Downtown Neighborhoods Association (Albuquerque)

At first glance Albuquerque seems to be little more than a large military-retirement-tourist city still booming while most of the nation suffers recession. It appears to have sprung anew out of a sun-kissed, mountain-bordered site, heavy on expressways and fast-food restaurants. Growth Town, USA. But no U.S. city has a longer, more dramatic history. In nearby Sandia Cave, evidence has been found of human occupation going back more than seventeen thousand years. In the fourteenth century Native Americans established pueblo communities, and in the sixteenth century Spanish conquerors arrived. U.S. troops moved in during the Mexican War in 1846, and never really left.

The railroad reached Albuquerque in 1880 but was resisted by the old town's mostly Spanish landowners, who foresaw drastic change. The depot and an Anglo-dominated new town were established two miles east. The new town prospered and grew as a transportation and commercial center, to become modern-day Albuquerque.

At the turn of this century the area between the old town and the new town began to fill in with a gridiron street pattern and homes and shops built in a variety of architectural styles. Anglo lawyers and merchants built fancy Victorian and Queen Anne houses in this "Downtown Neighborhoods" area, and in the 1920s less wealthy citizens constructed Midwestern bungalows. Small pueblo and Spanish adobe houses were put up by many Hispanics and a few Native Americans. In 1970 the area was 70 percent Hispanic, with median family income 60 percent that of the city as a whole.

In the 1970s, as the city boomed and new ranch house subdivisions blossomed in "the heights" of northeast Albuquerque, a few young professionals began to buy into the older Downtown Neighborhoods, attracted by the handy location and handsome old homes at bargain prices. In 1972 a handful of these middle-class newcomers and old settlers in Downtown Neighborhoods came together and formed Downtown Neighborhoods Association, the first Anglo neighborhood organization in Albuquerque. (There had long been loosely organized self-help organizations in some of the old barrios.)

The initial issue faced by the new association was a beautiful old home being considered for transformation into a drug rehabilitation center. A typical storm of protest was raised, with arguments made about possible saturation of the neighborhood by halfway houses. A deal was worked out with lawyers to have them acquire and restore the old home and use it as law offices. This was the first victory for the association, and it sent the organizers looking for more, with zoning laws and political pressure the chief weapons for preserving residential character and moving city government to provide some improvements.

While the organization protects housing and residents by fighting off commercial, apartment, and institutional encroachment, it also causes rents and housing prices to rise by upgrading and publicizing Downtown Neighborhoods as an "in" place to live. This dilemma is also being faced in Midtown in Wichita. No way has yet been found to make such organizational efforts displacement-proof.

Local businesses that do not maintain their property and businesses that want to expand into residential sections and cut down land available for single-family homes are considered a main threat to the neighborhood. But as well-heeled families, young professionals, and law firms seek to move in, gentrification and displacement loom as the most important issues. The incomes of some of the four thousand residents are over $40,000, but there are also residents on welfare. The association has a goal of restoration with a minimum of displacement, but this has been difficult to achieve in a city where growth dominates over decline.

The heart of the Downtown Neighborhoods Association is its fifteen-person board, whose members serve two-year terms. Seven or eight board members are elected each year from among ten to twelve nominees. An attempt is made to get a board mix that is geographically and ethnically representative and has both long-time residents and newcomers, but few Hispanics have taken an active role.

Active people are so few and committees so numerous that most committees have only one or two members, and some committees are inactive from time to time. However, the association has been able to generate citizen support for a project when the need arises. In 1979 Mayor David Rusk spoke with great respect for the accomplishments of the association and indicated a strong commitment by city government to help.

Neighborhood communication is maintained through a printed newsletter published four times a year. Neighborhood youngsters are paid to deliver the newsletter door to door, but it does not always get to every household. Copies are also left in stores. About a thousand copies of each issue are printed. There are a few block clubs in the neighborhood, such as Manzano Court, which cooperate with the association, and volunteers are recruited through these. The association would like to help build more block clubs.

One specific objective of the Downtown Neighborhoods Association is reopening of the area's public school, which was closed for lack of students. The association feels it cannot develop a first-rate neighborhood without a first-rate public school, with the size of the student body not a crucial factor. Said association leader Mary Beth Acuff, "Stability for our neighborhoods means families and families mean schools. . . . Not one more cent for suburban sprawl until we have the kind of exciting, urban, multilingual, multicultural primary school we deserve."

The association plays rough in attempting to run out absentee landlords who misuse and exploit their property. It harasses the owners directly to sell, calls police when any misconduct is noted on the property, and gets real estate brokers to make offers to the absentee owners. It calls out city inspectors on garbage violations, threatens public nuisance suits, and seeks to enforce the city's restrictive housing code against the property.

Another specific objective is to transform the principal street, Lomas Boulevard. This big, wide street moves straight through the middle of Downtown Neighborhoods, a typical heavily traveled, speed-when-you-can, dusty, polluted inner-city artery with a mish-mash of ugly stores, restaurants, gas stations, old houses, and vacant lots. The association developed a vision of Lomas as a handsome, leisurely boulevard with tall trees along the route, a textured surface, and new townhouses replacing the stores and gas stations. By late 1982 much of the beautification was under way, although most of the businesses remained.

The association was the first Albuquerque neighborhood organization to work with city planners in making a sector development plan. The area is being developed as the link between downtown and Old Town, now preserved as a historic area with San Felipe de Neri Church, built in 1706, its centerpiece. The plan is compatible with the association's emphasis on residential uses.

Much of the stimulus for organization and renovation in Downtown Neighborhoods has come from Jack Graham, a savings and loan banker, and Anna Muller, a prominent resident, who have not only supported the association but helped it persuade banks and city government to cooperate in sponsoring Neighborhood Housing Services (NHS) to help home owners to plan and finance repairs and improvements to their homes. The association has supported the NHS project since its beginning, and the two organizations share some board members.

The association is concerned about the nearby downtown and strongly supports its development, with more apartments along the edges, and more attractive shops. Disappearance of department stores and shops from downtown has gravely disturbed association leaders. "We don't want another sprawling Los Angeles or Phoenix with no true downtown focal point," says Acuff. The association is unusual in that its vision goes beyond the neighborhood to what the whole metropolis should be.

The association helped form a Coalition of Albuquerque Neighborhoods, along with twenty-five associations from other neighborhoods. The coalition works on problems of mutual concern to its member organizations.

Volunteer effort makes the Downtown Association go. There has never been paid staff and there is no plan to hire any. NHS does have staff members who give some help to the association; including assistance with the association newsletter. Talented professionals including bankers, lawyers, and journalists provide free help. The organization spends no more than a few hundred dollars a year, to print the newsletter and file zoning suits where court fees must be paid (but not the lawyers).

The association is very conscious of power and its importance to achieving objectives—both the power that comes from political pressure and the power that comes from money. It has realized the power of people when bringing large numbers to bear at zoning hearings. It has tasted the influence of money through the bankers who have assisted the neighborhood with its successful Neighborhood Housing Services.

Research has been used by the small, hard-working board, especially in building its case for the reopening of the school. The research efforts get at the number of children who might attend a high-quality, innovative elementary school, and the educational techniques that might be utilized. Generally the leadership cadre has a positive attitude toward research.

At the association's annual meeting there is a gripe table where residents fill out a form detailing a specific complaint. At an annual meeting, twenty-five or thirty forms might be filled out, all of them related to physical conditions of the neighborhood. These are presented to the city councilor for the area, who gets them to the proper city bureau. Two weeks after he receives the filled-out gripe forms the councilor reports back on his contacts with the bureaus.

The association makes a phone check to residents to see whether complaints are actually resolved. These complaints help the leadership determine the direction of the association program. The association works with the city each year on allocating federal Community Development Block Grant funds, which are used largely for basic improvements to streets, sewers, and arroyos (open storm sewers).

Overall, the influence of neighborhood associations with city hall rises and falls depending on the attitude of elected officials, who seem to change often in Albuquerque. By 1982 there were ninety-five associations in the growing city, with twenty-seven belonging to the Coalition of Albuquerque Neighborhoods. The coalition lost some of its influence and affiliated organizations when its president became a candidate for city council and resisted requests he step down as head of the coalition while campaigning.

In a growth city, Downtown Neighborhoods Association, with a strong leadership cadre, appears to have been important in the preservation and improvement of its neighborhood. It has done its work with little money. Now, as the local Neighborhood Housing Services expands (with an extra $90,000 in city community development funds in 1982), it tends to become the dominant, visible organization while the association, without staff and with few new dramatic issues to face, becomes less active and less visible. At the same time, it is secure in its record of having helped neighborhood people establish control over their own territory.

The Downtown Neighborhoods Association's achievement has come mostly through Anglo leadership. Not far away, in the old Barelas neighborhood, Hispanic leadership began building local influence much earlier.

Barelas Neighborhood Improvement Association (Albuquerque)

Barelas is in the valley on the southwest edge of downtown close to the Rio Grande. It is a community of twenty-five hundred families, most with quite modest incomes. Houses are small, crowded together, usually single-story adobe, many gray and weathered. Setbacks vary, and the irregular building lines give the area an informal appearance. Here and there is a small store or restaurant.

In years past this area of Hispanic people was loosely organized in traditional fashion with the leading families taking quiet initiatives to deal with government and other established systems on behalf of the people. The style of leadership was paternalistic. By 1959 some of the long-time residents had transformed this loose operation into the Barelas Neighborhood Improvement Association, with by-laws, a constitution, and a board of directors. The organizers were a cadre of five, and they moved the organization forward with collective leadership.

Over the years the organization had ups and downs, and authority gravitated to a single head of an established family, a *patrón* who "knew what was good" for the neighborhood. He came to ignore the board and by-laws, skipped elections, and made all decisions. In 1971 the *patrón* was challenged by younger, more contemporary heads of households. Elections resulted and more democratic leadership took over. The organization has grown in influence since then.

The Barelas Neighborhood Improvement Association pursues three goals: (1) to maintain cultural traditions of the area; (2) to utilize fully government programs for improved housing; and (3) to obtain the neighborhood's full share of other improvements and services from the city.

Consciously concerned with maintaining traditional values, social fabric, and sense of community, the Barelas Association carries on the time-honored Christmas pageant-play, *Los Posadas de Barelas,* the story of Mary and Joseph searching for an inn where Mary may give birth. Dozens of residents play roles, and hundreds attend. This festive community event has gone on for thirty-eight years. It is especially meaningful to Barelas's senior citizens, who make up almost half the population. In its programs, the organization is especially concerned about senior citizens. It has obtained a senior citizen center and government-aided housing, with more planned.

The Barelas Association is governed by a board of thirteen who are elected to one-year terms. An election is held every six months, with six or seven members elected each time. Officers are a president, vice-president, and secretary-treasurer, and they are elected once a year. No officer is supposed to serve more than two consecutive terms.

A major effort of the organization has been dealing with city and federal governments in the construction of an authentic Spanish-style housing development to serve the elderly. Instead of a large apartment building, there are several small clusters of single-story houses, each cluster built around a patio. Landscaping provides seating and shade areas. Leaders of the Barelas Association have insisted on traditional, small, ground-level houses as conducive to preserving the interrelationship, values, and life-style of the older people of Barelas. This project has been built on a prime piece of cleared land once blighted.

Responsibility for pushing the project has been carried by a special Senior Citizen Housing Problem Committee, which has also been concerned with loans to help elderly homeowners improve their houses. There are also a general housing problems committee and an activities committee.

The association has neither dues nor a formal budget. Money, services, and supplies are found as needed. The organization spends less than $1,000 a year, including the $400 spent on *Los Posadas.* Some funds come from sales of Hispanic food at festivals, and there is an occasional raffle. Usually the treasury has a balance of about $600. The organization is not eager to obtain grants, except for some senior citizen services. HUD once turned down its application for a solar heating demonstration grant.

Barelas people believe their tax payments entitle them to public improvements and services. The organization has pressed for repair and replacement of an inadequate sewer system. It has insisted that the city oversee housing rehabilitation to prevent shoddy work by contractors. It has sought to control zoning both to protect residential blocks and to secure needed commercial facilities. This includes vigilant monitoring of what happens to the vacant urban renewal land in the south section of the neighborhood. During the four years between 1979 and 1982, Barelas has been slated for over $9 million in improvements.

When the odor from a nearby sewer plant began to make life unpleasant for residents and discouraged private investment in Barelas, leaders of the association asked the city council for help, arguing that the plant was a waste of public funds and its odor an affront to taxpayers. Rebuffed by a foot-dragging council, Barelas turned to the county district attorney, who found three other neighborhoods affected also. He filed suit against the city, arguing that low-income neighborhoods were being discriminated against. The city government finally agreed to try to correct the nuisance. With the odor (and accompanying mosquitoes) pretty well gone, two restaurants and other businesses have opened nearby and more money has been invested in homes.

A major project of the activities committee was *el jardin publico,* a 114-plot public vegetable garden operated for several years on the vacant land where the senior citizen housing has now been built. Three kinds of plots were offered: family, senior citizen, and children's. The plots were well cared for, without vandalism or stealing. Much friendly interaction and helping developed among the plot holders, who were awarded certificates at an annual harvest dinner where some of the fresh produce was eaten. Slides of gardeners at work and their lush, maturing plants were shown.

Pat Turrieta was president of the association when the garden project reached its peak. He believes it not only contributed to the social fabric of Barelas, but helped people warm up to the urban renewal site and accept it as part of the neighborhood community. With the site now built upon, the association has tried other ways to promote gardening. It has run a workshop on how to garden, given away seeds and steer manure, loaned tools, and otherwise encouraged backyard plots. In 1983 it aims to have one or more new public sites available for gardening.

Gardening has been important to many for economic reasons. Prices rise, and few jobs are available for young people who do not learn technical skills or go to college, although Albuquerque's defense industry has protected it from the industrial layoffs affecting most other cities in 1982. However, as the city's economy grows steadily, young, educated Anglos benefit most. There has been substantial unemployment among Hispanics and Native Americans, but this is not new. Barelas people have always helped their neighbors in time of crisis. In 1982 a few families were doubling up in houses, and more youths were finding employment by joining the army, navy, or air force, but generally the neighborhood was no more hard-pressed than usual.

A monthly general meeting of the association draws 40 to 145 people, with 500 to 600 participating in at least one meeting, sponsored event, or activity during a year, not counting the large numbers viewing *Los Posadas* or stopping by the organization's booth at festivals. When a crisis threatens the neighborhood, the association seems able to turn out hundreds for a mass meeting or public hearing.

The Barelas association has no staff of its own but was assisted for years by the Barelas antipoverty office, now closed by the Reagan cutbacks. Some help on mailings is still available from the central antipoverty office, and the organization receives phone messages through the local community center. Association leaders see a benefit in the removal of staff help. "It makes us fall back on our own resources, we do more for ourselves," says Turrieta. "We always felt federal programs would be cut. There's always somebody willing to do our printing after hours in a neighborhood shop, or do other work that needs to be done. Barelas people appear to work as we need them. We are like the earthworm. One soon breaks into seven."

The organization tends to recruit people who are stable homeowners and remain in the leadership for years, becoming experienced and competent at many tasks, including cooperating in joint efforts with other organizations, negotiating with government, determining problems, and searching out solutions.

Leadership develops ideas and makes recommendations to the board on policy. The board screens ideas and presents them to membership meetings for final decision. Leaders and staff obtain some training by attending various kinds of locally offered workshops and conferences on urban renewal, legal aid, community development, neighborhood planning, zoning, and managing an organization.

The association assigns an officer or active member to keep in contact with each city, county, and state board, commission, and committee with powers or programs that could affect Barelas. Often the Barelas representative can present problems and information the government unit is unaware of, and persuade it to take action. Sometimes heavy pressure by way of a threat to withhold political support is necessary.

Members of the association have been appointed to some public boards and committees. Strength also comes from overlap between association leadership and leadership of the area's Democratic party committee. Most neighborhood organizations shun such arrangements, but the Barelas Association has found it quite useful; thus it leans a bit in the direction of an organization tied to politics. The leadership has respect for power and what power can produce. However, like all mature organizations, the Barelas Association is leery of the promises of elected officials and likes to get their statements in writing.

Evaluation is another tool used regularly. Reports made at board meetings are cast in a framework of: How well is the project going? What can be done better? What can be learned for next time? From evaluation the organization determines, in part, future programs, and learns which members can handle increased responsibility.

New members are recruited in tried and true manner, by word of mouth and personal contact by the leadership. Each project that succeeds gives the leadership a chance to sign up a few new members. Notices of membership meetings are sent widely throughout the neighborhood. Guest speakers on pertinent subjects and refreshments are used to help draw people to membership meetings.

Communications involve several media. A monthly flyer announcing the open meeting is circulated, sometimes carrying a news item of particular importance. A quarterly newsletter is distributed with articles about services offered and problems being handled by the organization's committees. Three free-standing, permanent bulletin boards have been constructed around the neighborhood. These carry news and notices from the association, plus individual notices posted by residents searching for a lost cat or seeking to sell a secondhand TV set. Volunteers keep an eye on the bulletin boards, removing stale material and ensuring that the boards remain neat and in good repair. Newspaper and TV publicity also are sought as often as possible.

The leaders believe government has been helpful to the neighborhood, and can be more helpful in the future. They find it pays to keep abreast of what local government is doing. They find government at all levels slow to act, and are convinced pressure is essential to get it moving. Participation of the organization's leaders in party politics probably indicates their faith in government.

The association has good relations with local business owners and managers. There is cooperation and mutual support, arising out of a shared interest in preserving and improving the neighborhood.

Joe Gonzales, current president, has sought to involve as many people as possible, and prevent any return of the *patrón* system. He and younger leaders feel that the greatest need of the organization is for more residents to understand that people gain power when they are united, and then they can get things done.

The Barelas Neighborhood Improvement Association sends a representative to meetings of the Coalition of Albuquerque Neighborhoods but has not formally joined. Leaders of the association are not yet convinced that the benefits warrant the payment of what they consider fairly high dues. The Barelas organization seems to be fiercely independent and proud, desirous of standing on its own feet. It also may fear domination by a coalition whose leadership is Anglo in a city where the population is down to less than 30 percent Hispano.

Fierce reaction came from the association when Anglo ACORN organizers flew in from the East and began to sign up senior citizens in Barelas, collecting 50¢ a week in dues. Turrieta led an angry effort to chase them out, asserting to the newspapers and district attorney that the outside organizers were intimidating old people. ACORN efforts ceased in Barelas but picked up in other low-income areas of Albuquerque.

A majority of the neighborhood's people belong to Sacred Heart Catholic parish, which cooperates with the association's efforts by announcing neighborhood meetings and projects. The church is a powerful element binding together the people of Barelas, as is the association.

The Hispanic factor is important to the Barelas Association's unity and pride, and to the neighborhood's sense of community. The association conducts its meetings and publishes its flyers and newsletters in Spanish and English. The organization has not hesitated to adopt contemporary Anglo methods of democracy, which in fact are compatible with the Hispanic tradition of *cabildo abierto* (open council), a process of shared decision-making found in the earliest Spanish settlements in North America. The organization is pragmatic, moving back and forth from pressure to service depending upon each situation. It probably can be said to have a mixed strategy.

Like the Hispanic culture in America, the Barelas Association seems destined to persist as it works to provide for well-being of its neighborhood. Steadiness and stability appear to be its chief traits.

Shadyside Action Coalition (Pittsburgh)

A much looser national network than ACORN's is formed by the neighborhood organizations tied to Saul Alinsky's venerable Industrial Areas Foundation. Roots of this network go back to the 1930s, when a youthful Alinsky, fresh from researching the organizing styles of radical unions and Chicago gangsters, began to experiment with techniques for organizing neighborhood people on Chicago's South Side. Alinsky perfected a method for getting results and then formed his foundation to teach the method to frustrated people in other cities. In forty years of struggle, the foundation has assisted dozens of urban neighborhoods to build strong organizations. However, it has never attempted to form them into a closely knit national coalition as ACORN has done. This case will describe the rise and fall of an Alinsky-oriented, militant approach organization in Pittsburgh.

Once a world leader among industrial cities, Pittsburgh came out of World War II aged, obsolete, and with an inferiority complex. A much-heralded civic effort known as the Pittsburgh Renaissance was launched to revive the city. The campaign concentrated on industrial, commercial, and institutional projects, including a new airport, high-rise office buildings, an arena with a retractable dome, expanded colleges and universities, and Three Rivers Stadium. Downtown and other highly visible parts of the city sparked up, and the economic base shifted, with fewer blue-collar jobs and more white-collar and professional jobs. These dramatic changes, together with the spectacular success of the Pirates and Steelers in Three Rivers Stadium, led Howard Cosell in 1979 to dub Pittsburgh "The City of Champions." Exit inferiority complex.

Broken into pieces by rivers and steep hills, Pittsburgh has long been a city of neighborhoods, many with an ethnic character. However, early Renaissance efforts did little to help the neighborhoods directly.

In the 1960s neighborhood people began to organize, and by the early 1970s there was at least one organization in each of the city's seventy-eight neighborhoods. One of the most active and controversial of these was the Shadyside Action Coalition, put together by an Alinsky-schooled organizer.

Shadyside is a highly diverse neighborhood, fifteen minutes from downtown. It has mansion-lined streets and a few back ways of deteriorated housing. It has large numbers of comfortable, modern apartments, some in high elevator buildings, many in remodeled charming old houses. There is heavy influence from nearby universities and colleges, with many students and faculty members living in Shadyside. Its main shopping street is a cluster of prosperous specialty shops and boutiques drawing customers from the whole county. In a few ways, it is a chic neighborhood. Single-person households are numerous. Childless households have increased and the population has dropped to below 14,000. As technical and professional jobs have multiplied in Pittsburgh, Shadyside has prospered much more than blue-collar neighborhoods hard hit by recession in steel and other manufacturing industries. The population is largely white with a scattering of blacks whose numbers are growing. Overall, Shadyside is a neighborhood of variety and vitality.

Its neighborhood organization was begun in 1973 by an experienced organizer from the outside named Bob Connolly. Connolly had been educated as a community organizer at the University of Pittsburgh and then received advanced training at the Industrial Areas Foundation. He was bent on initiating an Alinsky-type neighborhood movement in Pittsburgh. He launched his efforts in Shadyside because the local mental health program had promised the neighborhood a community organizer and was willing to pay his salary.

Following the Alinsky method, he spent months quietly interviewing visible and not so visible leaders in Shadyside. From each interview he collected more names. Gradually he came to know more about the neighborhood's potential leaders, and what was on their minds, than anybody in Shadyside. Carefully, he selected a cadre of people who were deeply concerned about the neighborhood, aware of some meaty issues, willing to give time, and able to draw in others. Heavy with clergymen, the cadre made plans to build an organization. Committees were set up to plan a structure and to develop issues. Additional people were drawn in to work on these committees. Existing agencies and institutions within Shadyside were cultivated, and residents in some subareas were assisted in forming block clubs. Out of this came a coalition of thirty-four organizations and agencies, most of them block clubs and churches, although it also included party political committees, a NOW chapter, a drug rehabilitation center, and a PTA.

From the beginning, SAC dealt with dramatic issues, including a notorious slum landlord, police action against burglaries, and future use of a large tract of publicly owned vacant land.

The coalition form provided quick access to money and people, with the organization having an institutional base from the beginning. The new organization was able to tap into existing strength. SAC appealed to the self-interest of existing institutions for survival in a city of declining population.

Under the SAC structure, each organization sent delegates to a monthly delegates council meeting where decisions were made, particularly as to what issues the organization would address. Each organization also sent ten delegates to an annual convention where officers were elected, constitution and by-laws established, and general program direction approved. Numerous committees worked on issues. These committees drew members from the whole population of Shadyside.

SAC flowered and won victories, and Connolly left to organize elsewhere, it being a principle of Alinsky organizers not to stay around long enough to tempt the organization into dependency. SAC signed a contract for staff service with a Pittsburgh Industrial Areas Foundation affiliate that Connolly had also helped to organize.

In time the five top officers of SAC came to make up a tight leadership core, gaining added legitimacy by bringing considerable money and numerous volunteers into the organization. The five came out of elite levels of churches, a real estate firm, and corporations. They worked hand-in-glove with the contracted Alinsky organizers. The staff role of the Alinsky organizers was reduced to advising the top leadership on strategy and training volunteers and lower-level leadership. A part-time secretary was retained for routine mailings and record-keeping.

SAC leaders felt there were two large advantages to purchasing professional staff services rather than employing their own staff. First, it cost less. Second, SAC could draw on a pool of leadership, utilizing various staff specialists as appropriate, such as a specialist in training, a specialist in research, and a specialist in media relations. Full-time staff was less important because some of the leaders were full-time institutional people with offices in the neighborhood. They were on the scene, and they had various institutional supports and time to give to SAC affairs. The five leaders came to feel their collective leadership was the real "organizer" within SAC.

At this time the organization was able to raise $12,000 to $15,000 a year, nearly all of it from within the neighborhood, and leadership was defined as those who could raise money and recruit people for actions, an action being a mass confrontation with some powerful agency, corporation, or individual from whom SAC wanted something. This way of operating gave the organization strong leadership but began to undermine the coalition structure. The organization shifted toward becoming an association of strong individuals rather than constituent organizations.

The tight core of leadership was hard-nosed and rigorous. It made large demands upon itself and upon others in the organization. This esprit de corps extended down from the top five leaders to the committee chairpersons and some of the delegates.

SAC leaders in their recruitment looked for angry individuals with a strong self-interest in maintaining and improving the neighborhood — usually property owners or institution officials. They saw self-interest and anger as essential to motivating people for arduous tasks of confrontation, fundraising, and recruitment. They felt that property owners were in the neighborhood to stay, while renters came and went. However, they found a few willing nonowners. By anger they meant indignation toward exploitation of the neighborhood by established forces, such as banks, local government, and irresponsible owners of rental property.

SAC placed great store on training. Three of its leaders attended two-week courses at the Alinsky-founded Industrial Areas Foundation training school in Chicago. A training specialist from Industrial Areas Foundation also traveled to Pittsburgh once a month to hold a training session for SAC activists, with the agenda suggested by SAC people.

In addition to this formal training there was much informal training. As an issue was worked on, volunteers were taught how to research the issue, how to plan a strategy, how to testify, and other skills. SAC leaders viewed skills as essential for effective participation. They also followed a habit of evaluation which contributed to learning. Leaders and staff were outspoken in assessing each other's work and that of potential leaders. After each action an evaluation session was held to learn from what had happened.

SAC sought to be the instrument through which Shadyside could control its own destiny, mainly by generating sufficient power to influence forces such as government planners, large property investors, banks, and school boards. SAC felt these forces had often been destructive to the neighborhood.

SAC carefully selected specific issues, staying away from broad, nebulous problems. The early issue on which SAC expended the greatest effort was the Fantastic Plastic night club. A former supermarket building on the edge of the neighborhood was elaborately remodeled by proprietors with alleged organized crime connections. The club lacked adequate parking facilities. It was located in a congested area with numerous apartments occupied by elderly people. Street noise and rowdiness generated by the club became a threat to people living nearby.

SAC organized massive public protest which denied the club a liquor license. It stimulated the mayor to withhold a dance permit. SAC backed nearby property owners in a zoning suit and built a strong case in the press against what it called "a massive gangster-controlled club" being located in a residential neighborhood that already had several establishments with liquor licenses. Strong pressure was put on the Mellon Bank, which served as trustee for the estate owning the building. The bank was asked to terminate the lease with the night club proprietors but refused to do so. A series of battles went on for over three years. Finally, unable to secure a liquor license or dance permit, the club closed.

Other issues given attention were the future use of a large piece of vacant land owned by the school board which sits next to a park and new school. The school board was inclined to hold on to the land for possible future school construction. SAC supported residents living near the site who wanted it returned to the residential use it once had. After long, heavy negotiations, the view of SAC and the residents prevailed, and the land was offered for sale to private developers who agreed to construct townhouses and apartments. High interest rates and shortages of construction money delayed the construction, and ground was not broken until May 1981.

SAC was deeply concerned about a proposal to construct express bus lanes on railroad right-of-way along one side of the neighborhood. Entry and exit ramps could put large numbers of buses on some of the quiet streets of Shadyside. Housing and zoning issues were continually given attention by the organization.

SAC followed a pressure strategy, as do all Alinsky-type organizations in their early years. It did not become involved in offering any direct services, leaving this to other organizations, some of which were members of the coalition. SAC was organized on the principle that becoming involved in services would distract it from its main work and could compromise its independence, since services require money from government, foundations, United Way, and other outside sources. SAC felt that accepting any such money would weaken the organization, making it dependent on the funding sources.

In pursuing their early objectives, SAC leaders followed Alinsky's "power-action" conflict approach. This involved identifying an enemy connected to each issue, preferably one from outside the neighborhood who had some control over the issue. Many times it would be an unseen enemy, like the Mellon Bank in the Fantastic Plastic case, whose "camouflage must be ripped away." On one issue several enemies might be identified. Enemies were not dealt with in polite discussions. They were negotiated with in hard bargaining sessions. SAC made an "action" out of each such session, assembling fifty to a hundred people with a self-interest in the issue. The enemy was forced to bargain in a threatening, unfamiliar crowd atmosphere. SAC tried to make no public move without a show of strength. The leaders carefully planned each move at a strategy session. Media attention helped SAC achieve influence, but its basic source of power was the participation and support of large numbers of people. SAC's claim to legitimacy, to be the true voice and conscience of Shadyside, rested on the active support of hundreds, sometimes thousands, of neighborhood people.

In its annual convention, its monthly delegate meetings, its planning sessions, and its actions, SAC showed it was an organization of large numbers, which needed no outside funds. Member churches contributed from their operating funds, block clubs held parties and dinners. SAC itself held central fundraising events, including a house tour of interesting homes and condominiums. Leaders got out and hustled contributions from individuals. For a while, a "Shadyside Survival Manual" was published which contained ads as well as phone numbers of where to call with a complaint about public services, or for help with a problem.

SAC relied heavily on research because the leaders felt that any large and important issue involves a set of opposing forces and that these cannot be known and assessed without carefully digging out the facts. When fighting the night club, SAC wanted to know who were the real owners and what were their possible connections to the governmental bodies that would make decisions about a liquor license and dance permit. It wanted to know who else might benefit from the club and what their relationships were. SAC leaders had a conspiratorial view of the world. They assumed that on any important issue there were likely to be invisible forces plotting to undermine neighborhood interests. When dealing with zoning problems, SAC sought to learn who owned the land affected, who held the mortgage, who were the attorneys for the owners, and what were the governmental contacts of both owners and attorneys. Patterns of land ownership were searched to see who might have a large vested interest in the neighborhood. Records of campaign contributions to local election officials were examined.

When there was to be an action, the people present at the planning meeting committed themselves to turn out a specific number of people for the action. Attendance was taken at each action. Those present were asked who had invited them so an accounting could be made on pledges. This was a major test for would-be leaders. Could they turn out people for an action? SAC found that the only effective way for one person to bring out another was a direct personal invitation by phone or in person.

SAC attracted and held people, in part, because of its militant conflict approach. There was an excitement in power. The organization sought effective people regardless of color. Its leaders felt that whites and blacks had been exploited by the same unseen forces and needed to work together against those forces.

SAC relied on meetings, telephone, and mail for in-house communication. For communication with the general public, the media were utilized as needed. SAC had no problem getting media attention since the issues it selected were important and dramatic. Large numbers of people turned out for action and mass meetings.

During the early years of SAC's existence, it considered itself an organization entirely outside government and party politics. It saw itself as an independent force, making sure government served the neighborhood well, and doing this as an organization of people with self-interests that were legitimate and moral.

Some of the leaders were suspicious of government. They felt that over the years the neighborhood had been harmed by government, in things government had done and failed to do. The school board tore down hundreds of homes for a great high school it never built; the city parking authority took many homes. Slum operators had been allowed to violate the law. Police protection had been inadequate. They often felt some unseen force defeated them in zoning cases. The organization therefore made restrictions against government officials holding office in SAC.

SAC leaders viewed participation as a means to an end. The end was power and control. Involvement of large numbers of people generated power.

What has been said so far covers the first four years of the organization. By 1977 most of the people involved in any particular issue seemed involved as supporters and researchers, while the decision-making seemed to stay largely with the top leaders. There was a process of decision-making in the series of research and strategizing sessions out of which actions on issues developed, and all taking part had a chance to influence the decision-making. But the top leaders, meeting weekly, with a broad view of the whole organization, largely determined the outcomes.

During 1977 some block clubs began to feel SAC did not serve their needs, and some had grown weary of the abrasive and less than democratic methods. The clergymen and business people in the top leadership felt at home with hardball power operations. They were used to them in their own jobs. It was the middle-class peace-loving types who found the power approach a problem. SAC's predilection for the jugular and for nondemocratic ways was offensive to these tolerant people. Also, they felt staff were not available to them, and that generally the problems on their blocks were being ignored.

Revolt spread throughout the ranks of the organization. Finally, a majority at a well-attended delegates council meeting voted to break the Alinsky connection and cancel the contract for professional staff service. It was an uprising of the membership that forced the top leadership to resign. The former officers took several member organizations with them and sought to form a rival coalition, but it never got going.

Since 1977, SAC has continued to push for Shadyside needs, but it has become a shadow of its old self. It lacks the discipline, the excitement, the high level of participation, and the power of the early years. It has begun to publish a monthly newsletter, and has improved internal communications. It has also given more people a chance to hold office. It still raises enough money for one staff organizer, but its actions are fewer and less militant.

In the 1980s the organization's more democratically inclined leadership made other changes in structure and strategy. In 1981 the SAC constitution was amended to provide that a resident may join as an individual member, but only for one year. After the year, the member has to belong through a block club or other organization. If there is no block club in the member's area, SAC will help the member form one.

In late 1982 SAC was very much alive, with its efforts centered on preservation. It was giving strong support to block clubs developing anticrime "block watches" in cooperation with the local police. An active housing and zoning committee was laboring to maintain high standards in the uses of land and quality of structures. SAC was important to its neighborhood and had productive relationships with city hall, but it was no longer the city's most powerful neighborhood organization.

Northwest District Association (Portland, Oregon)

Portland, Oregon, is located in a region where people care a great deal about their environment. Neighborhoods are treated with respect and lavished with attention, with considerable direct assistance provided to neighborhood organizations by city government.

A short distance to the west of Portland is the Pacific Ocean, connected to the city by the wide and beautiful Columbia River. To the east are snow-topped Mounts Jefferson and Hood. Vast green forests cover much of the region. But in 1982 the once flourishing lumber industry was fading as housing construction collapsed nationally. Unemployed workers drifted into the city.

Portland's downtown is big and impressive. It has kept its department stores and retail shops, and its renovated streets have textured surfaces, special lanes for buses, and handsome benches, planters, and bus passenger shelters on wide sidewalks. Rising unemployment throughout the region has been hurting downtown, however, and retail sales are down.

Portlanders for a long time have responded to their environment with love and affection. They have cherished it and cared for it, and passed laws to protect it. This has carried over to preserving the neighborhoods, which also now feel the threat of recession. In the neighborhoods, lush rose bushes bloom unmolested at curbsides. Litter goes into containers. Well-designed phone booths stand on corners unvandalized. Transit buses run frequently on neighborhood streets, on schedule, at modest fares. And the poor elderly sign up for free cheese.

Neighborhood organization began in Portland in the 1930s around concerns about juvenile delinquency. Victory gardens provided a coalescing activity during World War II. Most groups melted away after the war, though. Beginnings of the current network of neighborhood organizations came in the late 1960s along with the civil rights and anti-Vietnam movements, in which ordinary citizens began to stir and assert their interests. It was a time of prosperity and growth in Portland, and some of the industrial corporations and large institutions located in neighborhoods began to expand, threatening residential blocks. One neighborhood where expansion plans provoked reaction was Northwest, a particularly well-cared-for old neighborhood of frame houses and vital street life centered on the shops and restaurants of Northwest Twenty-third Street.

A growing hospital in Northwest's center, and an expanding national trucking firm located at the edge, both wanted more land, and eyed some of the neighborhood's old housing. They asked the city government to clear houses through urban renewal. Residents mobilized spontaneously against this effort and blocked it by mass protest. Soon these residents were also fighting a freeway proposal aimed at their neighborhood, and were winning that one, too. They persuaded government to modify the corridor, resulting in less impact on the neighborhood.

This organized effort at protection brought into being the Northwest District Association. Established in 1969, the association developed a broad program including public improvements. In time it hired a part-time staff organizer, Mary Pederson, a restless college professor with a Ph.D. in political science who lived in the neighborhood and was looking for a new way to practice the political science profession. With her staff leadership, residents built their Northwest District Association into one of the first important post-1960s neighborhood organizations in Portland.

Northwest District Association developed a board of sixteen elected at an annual general meeting and three co-chairpersons as top brass: one for administration, one for social action, and one for planning and land use. This troika spread around the status, involved more people, and reduced burnout of top leadership. The organization used three-headed leadership to make it possible for the chairpersons to concentrate on their areas of greatest strength, since few people are competent in all areas.

The board now has small committees on planning and land use, traffic and transportation, parks and recreation, social concerns, economic development, and communications. About two thousand of the neighborhood's fifteen thousand people are members. Membership is open to anyone who lives, works, or owns property in the neighborhood of two and a half square miles. To vote in the annual election, a member is required to be registered. The board meets three times most months, and its actions and statements make news, often in the neighborhood newspaper, sometimes citywide. Staff make recommendations to the board, and often have considerable influence.

Committee members and candidates for the board are recruited mainly from those who respond to an issue or crisis. A few just appear at the office with ideas (some good, some bad). The storefront office on busy Northwest Twenty-third Street has been found to be a useful central point where things happen and people keep dropping in.

The Northwest Association provides orientation for new board members at the first meeting of each organizational year, and has an annual potluck supper at which board members discuss priorities for the future. Some evaluating goes on at this meeting as board members talk about where they have been and where they are going. The association maintains a won-lost book on land use fights.

One major issue involved developers who took out a building permit for an apartment building, and then began building a motel. The association mobilized five-hundred angry residents at a mass meeting, where city officials promised the new housing would be limited to rental apartments. When the building was completed, the association found it being advertised and used as a motel. Follow-up resulted in a lawsuit being filed against the city.

The association is principally a pressure organization, although heavy demands are made upon it to develop services. In past years, it has initiated some social services but spun them off to a new Northwest Service Center which it helped to organize. The center has been struggling to cope with increased demands for food, clothes, jobs, and housing help from the unemployed, including Asiatic boat refugees as well as jobless lumber workers and unskilled youth.

There is strong awareness of the need for power to be able to apply effective pressure. Some members become active in political campaigns, as individuals, but with an aim of enhancing neighborhood power. A staff coordinator, Margaret Strachan, resigned in 1979 to become an aide to a city commissioner and in 1980 was herself elected to that powerful office.

Money was a problem until 1974 when original staff organizer Pederson joined with the leaders of other young neighborhood groups to persuade city government to establish the Office of Neighborhood Associations. Mary Pederson left Northwest Association to head this new bureau which began to provide staff, office space, and other help for neighborhood organizations.

The Northwest District Association now shares a staff and headquarters with five other neighborhood organizations. It raises a small amount of additional money for special projects such as a tool bank. Margaret Strachan, who became Northwest's city-paid staff coordinator after Pederson moved downtown, wanted to give token salaries to volunteers who put in twenty hours a week or more, but never had the money.

The association believes in research, and has used surveys to learn about needs for parks and recreation facilities, and to ascertain attitudes on housing. A professor from the neighborhood helped design the housing questionnaire, which was administered by CETA workers and volunteers and proved quite useful. In 1979, the association carried out a displacement survey which revealed the dimensions of that process and guided the design of a program to slow it down. The association finds research generates new programs and more needs for funds, and is useful in making demands on city government.

The association communicates with members mainly through one-page announcements rather than a regular newsletter. Much information is placed in *The Neighbor,* a local commercial newspaper circulating five thousand copies per week. Three times a week *The Oregonian,* a daily newspaper, carries neighborhood news, with its staff accepting information over the phone. Cable television has recently come to Portland, with access available to community groups. Geri Ethen, coordinator of the Northwest office in 1982, said this about the potential of cable television for the neighborhood associations:

> We have already used cable television for twelve neighborhood shows on important issues. The audiences aren't real big yet, but we probably reach more people than we do at meetings. There is a problem getting access to the studio and equipment, and producing a show is tough for volunteers—a lot of time and skills are needed to be effective. But we feel cable TV has real potential and we'll stick at it.

The association's cooperative stance toward city government carries over to its attitude toward business and industry, with a "that's what makes the city go" attitude. In the Oregon spirit of fairness, the association feels no large group, including public officials and corporation executives, can be cast as evil.

Since city government began funding offices and staffs, Northwest Association has shared its office and staff with the Northwest Industrial Neighborhood Association, made up of trucking, warehousing, and fabricating companies in the nearby industrial section. It is unique in Portland and is one of few such organizations in the United States. The Industrial Association began in the early 1970s at the time of the freeway route battle. The companies had a vital stake in the route, and felt, prior to organizing, that no one was representing their interest. The companies wanted to speak with a single voice.

Possessing able leadership and a limited program, the Industrial Association does not demand much from the staff, but is given help as needed. Sometimes conflict over an issue develops between the industrial area and residential neighborhood. Then the staff brings together leaders from the residents' associations and the industrial association, and they try to negotiate a compromise before open battle begins. The staff has found that industrial and residential neighborhood leaders can usually work out a solution.

When Pederson stepped up to direct the Office of Neighborhood Associations in 1973, she helped divide the city into five large sections, each with a set of whole neighborhoods. The Northwest office expanded to become headquarters for the neighborhood associations in its section. Similar joint offices were set up in the other four sections of the city.

Pederson's first-year budget was $104,000 from hard tax funds. Portland's nonpartisan city government, led by Mayor Neil Goldschmidt, never viewed the burgeoning network of neighborhood groups as a political threat as did partisan governments in some of the cities of the East and Midwest. An unusually productive relationship between city hall and neighborhood organizations seems to prevail in Portland. The budget rose to $332,500 in 1980, when organizing citizen participation in community development became an added responsibility. Neighborhood based anticrime programs were added in 1982, with the budget reaching over $500,000.

Each of the five section staffs and offices serves the recognized neighborhood organizations in its section. To be recognized and eligible to share in use of an office, an organization must open its membership rolls to all neighborhood people, collect dues only on a voluntary basis, and provide its members with formal processes for dissenting on a decision or filing a grievance against the organization. Elected officials have thus sought to ensure that no eligible citizen is ever excluded, and that minority rights are protected within neighborhood organizations. Under Mary Pederson's leadership, the number of recognized organizations grew steadily to over fifty by late 1979, including organizations made up of neighborhood business people.

When a neighborhood organization makes a request or recommendation to city government, the dissenting views of any member must be included in writing. Each organization must have a written procedure through which any member may request reconsideration of a decision. A copy of the by-laws of each recognized organization is kept on file in the Office of Neighborhood Associations.

Neighborhood associations participate in the hiring of staff for their section offices. In a section the recognized associations each appoint a representative to serve on a section review board. The review board interviews candidates for top staff positions in the section office and recommends a candidate to the appropriate elected city commissioner, who approves the final hiring. Appropriate preparation for the job seems to be experience as a volunteer and as operator of a complex activity, such as running a political campaign or managing a small business.

Each joint review board negotiates an annual budget with the Office of Neighborhood Associations, oversees the operation of its office, and sets the work program for the staff. All of this is spelled out in an agreement between the Office of Neighborhood Associations and each review board. When an agreement and budget have been worked out between a review board and the Office of Neighborhood Associations, the city advances the review board an initial $5,000. It spends from the fund, makes monthly reports, and is reimbursed for expenditures, so it has a constant $5,000 fund from which to pay for its office and staff.

At least once a year each review board meets with staff of the city office to appraise the previous year's effort, evaluate district staff, and take up any other relevant matters.

The city office offers training for neighborhood staff and volunteer leadership. Training sessions, workshops, and conferences have been held on subjects from landuse planning, economic development, cable and computer technology to leadership and organizational development. Through arrangements made by the city office, section staff get informal training from the Internal Revenue Service and the Oregon State Revenue Department on financial record-keeping. A city auditor regularly visits the five offices to give further direction on financial management.

The downtown office furnishes forms to staff which they use with their neighborhood organizations to list project goals (such as getting a street paved or day-care service expanded) and process goals (more people participating, increased publicity). Every three months tally sheets go downtown showing progress toward goals.

In September of each year, neighborhood organizations submit "needs forms" for public services and capital improvements required for their areas. The city office sorts these and forwards them to the proper bureaus, later following up to ensure they are given attention. An annual score sheet is published, with about 40 percent of requests met.

Although the city office pushes the bureaus for action, it seeks to avoid doing their work for them. Occasionally, the office pulls together two or more bureaus to make a plan for meeting a complex request. One of these was to save several historic sequoia trees which were interfering with curb and sidewalk improvements in an old neighborhood.

Every month downtown administrative staff meets with the five section coordinators, talking over matters that affect two or more neighborhoods. Part of the meeting is given over to listening to a city bureau head or civic official with a new idea or program to discuss. The Office of Neighborhood Associations has become a clearinghouse for innovations, and an exchange for success stories.

Experience shows it takes six months for a section coordinator to get on her feet and operate effectively. So far, coordinators have not had to be concerned about fundraising, but this arduous task may lie ahead. The coordinator position is a tough one, with high public visibility. People not good at the job do not stay long. But a good one, like Margaret Strachan, rises to elective office.

The city Office of Neighborhood Associations has helped many new associations come into being and continues to provide assistance to individuals and groups wishing to organize. Citizens usually come for help when they face a crisis over some pressing need or issue. If forming a new organization seems appropriate, the city office will furnish flyers and meeting notices, and advise on how to proceed. When a group of people is ready to form a permanent association, staff will attend the initial organizing meeting to describe the methods used by other associations. Staff sticks with the group through the months of planning and open meetings needed to bring a solid organization into being. When issues related to city governmental services are raised, staff arrange for appropriate personnel from the city's operating bureaus to participate in the meetings. One of the principal ongoing functions of the city office is to facilitate working relationships between city bureaus and neighborhood organizations.

Besides advice on organizing and on writing by-laws, the Office of Neighborhood Associations gives neighborhood associations help in planning projects and putting out a newsletter. Each association is allowed twelve legal-size pages of newsletter printing per year, which means one page for a monthly, or three pages for a quarterly.

In the past, the city contracted with associations for the operation of youth service centers and currently has contracts for neighborhood based anticrime programs. The latter have become more important as young out-of-work transients flow into some neighborhoods where they mug and steal to survive. Several associations may be involved in one contract, with a joint board set up to oversee the service, but with budget control remaining in the hands of city council. Associations are free to raise additional funds to enlarge the service in any way they see fit. In 1982 some associations were getting new pressures for life-sustaining services including food, clothing, jobs, and housing. One had opened a "clothes closet."

Northwest District Association in 1982 had a line of job seekers passing through its office, only a few of whom it could help, and those informally. It did become a local deliverer of government cheese and fuel assistance. It found the displacement issue disappearing as people doubled up in housing. State government budget-tightening resulted in more mental patients being turned into the neighborhood from public institutions, generating new pressures for cheap housing, and providing more vulnerable marks for muggers. Welfare cutbacks were pushing thousands of Asian refugees off welfare, causing rising racial friction in Portland neighborhoods. The responsibilities of neighborhood organizations grew with the recession. Basic survival needs began to occupy more time and energy of the section offices and their affiliated associations.

At the same time, in an interesting, attractive neighborhood like Northwest, there was the lurking fear in the minds of the association's leadership that if interest rates came down and the economy began to recover, a great new wave of housing displacement would suddenly occur with elderly people, former mental patients, and Asian refugees tossed to the winds.

Portland's government has made an unusually large commitment to neighborhood organization. Probably nowhere else has collaboration been so dominant between neighborhoods and local government. And in a decade of budget retrenchment by local governments almost everywhere, Portland's Office of Neighborhood Associations keeps growing, with a budget to match the growth. Seemingly, only a deepening depression could slow it down. In 1982 there was such a possibility.

Patti Jacobsen, director of the Office of Neighborhood Associations in 1982, spoke of the maturing neighborhood-city relationship as "co-production" and saw it becoming a permanent component of Portland's public life. In 1982, seventy-four associations were served by the five section offices under her direction.

While Portland's underwriting of neighborhood organizations with staffs, offices, and services looks like a big-budget operation, each individual organization, such as the Northwest District Association, has a relatively small budget, depends in large part on volunteers, and usually sticks to a pressure strategy. Coordinator Geri Ethen of Northwest feels that the association would survive even if all city supports were withdrawn: "It would be at a smaller scale, it would drop some programs and focus on land use issues, maybe even raise enough funds locally for a half-time staff member. Too many neighborhood people realize the need for the association to let it die. They just care too much about their neighborhood."

Comment

The organizations described in this chapter make great use of volunteers and pressure. They confirm once more that much can be accomplished with little money, even in an era of recession and unemployment.

Through each of these organizations, neighborhood people have increased their power to determine the quality of life in their own communities. Besides achieving a degree of self-governance for their communities, these organizations have strengthened social fabric by cementing relationships among people. They have shown that city governments can and will respond to organized groups of neighborhood people, who happen to be voters, and that influence with city government gives a neighborhood organization some control over economic forces such as the real estate interests in Wichita and the hospital in Portland. These small-budget organizations also reveal weaknesses which flow from lack of skills, information, resources, and will.

Unrealized potential is revealed in the cases. Volunteers in Wichita's Midtown have generated the clout to ban trucks from their interior streets, but have not created a training program to develop fully their own talents as organizers. Albuquerque's Anglo and Spanish residents have separately organized to preserve their neighborhoods, but have not become actively allied to achieve even more. Pittsburgh's once powerful Shadyside Action Coalition no longer seeks to dramatize big issues, but has slipped into a preservation mode. And residents of Greensboro's Arlington Park neighborhood have been divided and conquered, although achieving some of their goals in the process.

The low-budget pressure organizations pictured here require a constant supply of enthusiastic volunteers willing to improve their skills. As long as the organizations deal with issues touching people's real concerns, they seem able to attract the volunteers. Most of the organizations in this chapter have demonstrated an ability to do short-term crisis recruiting. When some exciting crisis issue arises, the leadership cadres of these organizations spread the word by flyer, through media, word-of-mouth, and other means. Sizable numbers of people whose interests seem affected respond. Mass meetings are held. Power is demonstrated. The battle is won. And the crowds disappear.

The organizations have found it difficult to retain new people as active members. Where new recruits have been retained, it is benefits that retain them. They are accepted and treated well by the "old" cadre members. A personal relationship is established that is pleasurable and therefore a benefit. Or recruits may merely be shown that continuing to work with the organization can help achieve an objective they desire. Or a specific material benefit may be offered. (The Barelas recruit may want a garden plot, or the Shadyside block club may want help controlling a home for delinquent teen-agers.) It is the age-old matter of incentives.

Once the recruit makes a beginning commitment, training becomes important so the new member can have some skills and feel competent and successful. Few of the organizations have systematic training programs.

Beyond the need for attention to incentives and training, the organizations have taught a useful lesson about dealing with elected public officials. The experience of these organizations is that you don't worry about offending elected city officials. They'll always respect your numbers.

The media will respect both your numbers and your careful research, and will enlarge your power in the eyes of officials once you win their respect.

Honest pressures, reflecting the true desires and needs of neighborhood people, appear useful to city government. They help direct its limited resources to the most efficient uses, just as buyers in the marketplace help direct private firms to produce the most needed goods and services. Some elected public officials seem to recognize this useful function performed by pressuring neighborhood organizations.

As neighborhood organizations can direct government and other outside forces in what they do for the neighborhood, the more self-governing the neighborhood community becomes, the more likely its people's needs are to be met, and the more easily it wards off decline and achieves stability.

In spite of their weaknesses, the organizations described in this chapter have all achieved some level of success. In part, this has been possible because they have had persistent cadres of leaders, and because their neighborhoods are not slums. They are not overwhelmed by deterioration. The neighborhoods in these case studies are sound—in need of protection and improvement, to be sure, but with many well-cared-for homes, stable families, and developed social relationships.

Although these six neighborhood organizations use proven methods such as mass meetings and newspaper publicity to protect and improve their communities, they do seem to need systematic recruiting and training to keep their organizations strong. Likewise, the organizations probably could benefit from more regular evaluation sessions, where members would examine critically what they have been doing.

As these organizations press for change, sometimes substantial change, they are very much a part of the traditional American system, and their efforts strengthen that system. They seem only to be using law and democratic processes to preserve local community. They are not in any sense radical organizations.

Although the strategy of the six organizations is primarily pressure, all seem to be pushed and tempted toward sponsoring a service or two. Shadyside Action Coalition and the Arlington Park Neighborhood Organization have resisted the temptation. The Shadyside organization does sponsor an anticrime watch, but this seems largely a device to keep pressure on the police. Northwest District Association, Midtown Citizens Association, and Downtown Neighborhoods Association have helped to start services but made sure they were housed in separate nonprofit corporations. Barelas Neighborhood Improvement Association has had ties to antipoverty and senior citizen programs, and has become involved in services. All of the groups, over time, are likely to move from pressure to a mixed strategy of pressure and services.

None of the organizations raises much money, but all require at least a small amount of staff help. Largely, they seem resourceful at obtaining staff from other organizations such as an antipoverty agency, city government, Neighborhood Housing Services, or a national organization such as ACORN.

The economic recession of 1981-82 seems not to have slowed them, since they are much more dependent upon volunteer energy than upon money. Seemingly they could flourish in the deepest depression.

5. Case Studies II:
Big-Budget Service and Economic Development Organizations

A small but increasing number of neighborhood organizations go out and raise large sums of money to become producers of services and goods rather than pushers and pressurers. Usually such organizations start with a few volunteers and work their way to a service strategy and a big budget. They acquire money for starting their own service programs and setting up neighborhood economic development projects. Sometimes they do much to build the strength of their neighborhoods. But their size and their dependence on outside resources bring difficulties.

We will now look at six such organizations and see some of their specific strengths and difficulties. The first big-budget organization is in Baltimore.

Southeast Community Organization (Baltimore)

Although it lies 170 miles up Chesapeake Bay from the Atlantic Ocean, Baltimore since its founding in 1729 has been a great port city shaped and influenced by low-cost water transportation. The *Baltimore Clipper,* built there and used throughout the world, was one of the great sailing vessels of all time. Diverse manufacturing and sophisticated services like medicine and education have also helped make Baltimore an important city.

A few decades back, in the heyday of the central cities, Baltimore's population approached one million. It has since fallen below 800,000, leaving it still one of the top ten U.S. cities. The city divides into several large, important sections. One of the oldest and most important of these is Southeast.

Sprawling Southeast Baltimore includes much of the historic innerharbor and encompasses many small neighborhoods. The population of 90,000 is a polyglot of races and nationalities, income levels, and life-styles. Modest-income white working people predominate, although a fifth of the population is in poverty, and a tenth is black.

Large numbers of residents walk to work at factories, warehouses, hospitals, and wholesale and retail businesses. Many ethnic groups—Polish, Ukrainian, German, Finnish, Irish, Czech, black, Appalachian, and Lumbee Indian—lay claim to at least one neighborhood. Like most industrial sections, Southeast has been suffering increased unemployment.

Neighborhoods settled and named one to two centuries ago exist today and house some of the descendants of original residents. The Fells Point neighborhood traces its roots back to 1726, three years before the founding of the city.

From 1966 to 1971 there was a flurry of sporadic organizing efforts in Southeast neighborhoods, aimed to stop an expressway, meet serious youth and senior citizen needs, save historic sections, and block the closing of a branch library. Out of these and similar activities to preserve community life in Southeast sprang a new interneighborhood coalition of organizations, calling itself Southeast Community Organization (SECO).

Since 1970 SECO, with its coalition structure, has become powerful and has spawned an array of programs, but with periodic swings in strategy. It is a dramatic example of an organization that began with a pressure strategy, moved into services and economic development, and finally found itself pushed back to pressure activities by the demands of neighborhood people, as well as by the need for a visible power base from which to bargain with government and the private sector for support for development and services. At the present time the pressure and service strategies are in balance.

SECO is a coalition organization: a federation of block clubs, improvement and civic associations, senior citizens groups, church groups, and planning councils. By 1980, member groups numbered over seventy and reflected a multiplicity of interests and population within Southeast Baltimore. Each member organization handles its own small issues, but looks to SECO for help on large issues.

A complex structure has emerged. An annual congress, composed of delegates from each member group, decides long-range policy questions and elects the officers of the organization. From month to month, short-range policy is made by a senate composed of one representative from each member group in the federation. And from week to week, decisions are made by an eleven-person executive committee, also elected by the congress.

From the beginning, SECO sought to find and involve leaders, neighborhood people with some following. During its first organizing drive in 1971, the long-time visible leaders of the Southeast community came to organizing meetings. But early on, some of these traditional position holders began to drop out of the SECO effort, seemingly because numerous people participating democratically scared them, somehow made them afraid they would lose their leadership status.

One of the young activists who moved to fill the leadership vacuum was Barbara Mikulski, who took the initiative to help launch SECO and then got herself elected to city council, and eventually to Congress, where she has become an effective and well-known member. In the early 1970s, SECO used the "rising star" technique in promoting her, and gained some advantage from her political advancement. More recently, SECO has taken an independent position toward Mikulski and works with her as it does with any other politician.

As SECO was being formed in 1970, the organizing cadre hired Joe McNeely, who had worked with a variety of urban groups in several cities. He shared the cadre's vision of big plans and large accomplishments, and became their full-time organizer. McNeely began by telling the cadre he needed fifteen volunteers who could give him fifteen hours a week. Twenty-five were forthcoming, and the Southeast area was divided into subareas with each volunteer organizer assigned to a subarea. These volunteer organizers came to understand that they had to focus on finding leader types—that is, neighborhood people with influence and some following.

The twenty-five formulated a plan to have a meeting in three weeks at which their members would double to fifty, three weeks later from fifty to one hundred, then to two hundred, and so on. The projected number for the founding congress to be held in the spring of 1971 was a thousand people. The volunteer organizers succeeded in recruiting fifty for the first session. At the second gathering it rained, and only sixty people came instead of the projected hundred. At the third meeting there were two hundred.

As meeting attendance grew, political officeholders began to appear: city council members, state representatives, and the like. Instead of being given the usual chairs at the front table, these officials were seated among the people. They were allowed to speak only under the same rules governing other community persons present.

The crowds drew press attention and helped build public interest in the founding congress of SECO, which was held April 7, 1971, with one thousand people participating. Ralph Nader appeared as keynote speaker. Task forces were set up to deal with several issues such as education, social problems, social services, health, the ever-present expressway plan, and housing.

The health task force took on the city and state to stop them from closing a hospital facility caring for chronically ill senior citizens, many from the Southeast area. Negotiations were launched with the mayor and governor, the governor's mansion was picketed, and a huge organizing effort resulted in a mass meeting at the Civic Center in downtown Baltimore with senior citizens from throughout the city participating.

SECO won the fight, and the facility was kept open. The organization counts this as a crucial victory for a number of reasons. First, it confirmed for the small organizations and individuals who participated in the founding congress that SECO could generate power and win a major victory. Second, it was a learning experience under fire for new leaders, who gained confidence in themselves. Third, it demonstrated the strength of a coalition structure. Fourth, it forced public officials to take the new organization seriously. Finally, it increased the interest of potential funding sources.

Other battles were quickly joined, as an outside grant was obtained for two full-time organizers. These organizers assisted the task forces which were attempting to build programs. The task forces that took up specific issues affecting many people flowered, won victories, and gained a sense of accomplishment. Those without specific issues floundered. Issues undertaken by the more effective task forces involved truck traffic through the neighborhood, vandalism and fighting in a park, and locations for two new schools.

Although these issues were handled largely through a pressure strategy, certain needs catching the attention of the organization called for a service strategy. Needs were identified for special reading classes for dyslectic children, a health services co-op, and a recycling center. All of these services were established. (The recycling center was short-lived due to lack of wide support.)

SECO staff and volunteer leadership began to feel that both pressure and services could help the organization get important things done. They began to look more into services. Their outside funding source, the National Center for Urban Ethnic Affairs, sent staff members to discuss the possibility of SECO's sponsoring a community development corporation, which might provide both human services and neighborhood-controlled businesses.

As SECO moved toward a community development program, a series of five Saturday workshops was held to allow neighborhood groups to learn about community development corporations, how they are structured, how they work, and how SECO groups could participate in planning a corporation and benefiting from its operation. This five-session training effort also became a planning process in which community leaders moved toward definite decisions on the type and kind of community development programs they might undertake.

After much soul-searching by leadership and receipt of a Ford Foundation community development planning grant, a new corporation was created, Southeast Development, Inc. (SDI). The SECO senate members became the members of the new corporation. They set up a Southeast Development board, made up of the executive director of SECO, an officer of SECO, and nine others chosen by the annual congress. Seven of these nine were required to live in Southeast Baltimore. While following goals set by the SECO senate, the development corporation board from the beginning has made its own month-to-month decisions.

A policy was early established to create a separate board to govern each new service and economic development project. Whenever the Southeast Development board would consider a potential project, it would consider not only social and economic needs, but also the existence of a readily identifiable constituency from which a project board might be drawn.

Southeast Development moved quickly to help create a neighborhood housing services corporation to aid home owners in property renovation, a primary health care corporation, a clothing design and manufacturing corporation, a much-needed local supermarket, a commercial revitalization program, a land bank, and a metal craft firm. Other arms of SECO reached into youth services and aid to families.

Meanwhile, an organizing staff was still working with a variety of member groups on issues that required a pressure strategy. SECO's lead organizer used an aggressive Alinsky confrontation approach in these efforts.

Before the service programs developed, there had emerged a philosophical opposition to moves into service delivery and economic development. The lead organizer, Stan Holt, opposed a service and development strategy. His Alinsky style increasingly conflicted with the dominant SECO approach, which was one of friendship and discussion, with militant action a last resort.

The tension forced a decision when Holt's contract came up for renewal. Early in SECO's history, harmony among member groups had become the operating method. Holt had been using confrontation tactics to generate competition and hostility among member groups for the purpose of turning out large numbers at meetings. The tactic generated crowds, but it began to erode what many SECO leaders felt was an essential unity. The time came for the senate meeting where Holt's future with SECO was to be decided. His supporters, who favored a pressure strategy and conflict approach, sought to mobilize senate members on their side. Those who wanted to continue the service and economic development strategy, and the cooperative approach, mustered their supporters.

The senate meeting was tumultuous, with a majority of votes going against contract renewal. The organizer stalked out and took many of his senate supporters with him. But their ensuing efforts to form a strong rival organization based on a pure pressure strategy failed. The split hurt SECO because, as a coalition, it lost not merely a few individuals but whole organizations. Nonetheless, the split gave a further impetus to program development. And SECO gained a certain focus by moving in that direction.

The SECO coalition entered a period of fence-mending and rebuilding, with services, fundraising, economic development projects, recruitment, and training receiving major attention. The organization became more concerned with coordination and administration, internal maintenance and repairing. It became bureaucratic.

As the rebuilding took place, the Southeast Development Corporation continued to expand its program, and its own board took more initiative to create new projects. SECO, through the powers of its senate and executive committee, retained the right to set policy for the corporation to ensure that its services and business ventures met the neighborhood's needs. As the body with a mass base, SECO had felt it was better able to do this than the corporation itself, with its small, elite board. But as the corporation grew and its projects proliferated, its small board faced more frequent and more complex decisions, and it inevitably began to do some of its own planning and policy-making.

SECO was preoccupied with rebuilding after the split and moved to prove itself with new programs and increased resources. More research was undertaken, with special grants obtained for the purpose. Human service programs expanded. Counseling services for youth were extended. Employment-manpower services began. Full-time staff increased to twenty-five, plus VISTA volunteers and student interns from local colleges. SECO's annual budget rose to $220,000. Staff, together with a small group of the long-time stable, less militant officers, came to dominate the organization. They were concerned with maintaining the internal organization, with administration, and with harmony. Pressure activities tapered off. Senate meetings declined, and the annual congress became smaller and less dramatic.

By 1979 this movement toward development and bureaucratic isolation led to new internal conflict. Staff members, senate members, officers, volunteers, and member organizations began to raise objections and make demands. Some felt the development corporation was becoming too independent and needed to be pulled back under the SECO wing. Others felt the corporation needed more autonomy to be efficient. There were cries for wider participation of residents in running SECO. And individual neighborhood organizations wanted more attention paid to their immediate needs, which would require that SECO get back to pressure activity.

As the storm intensified, the staff directors of both SECO and the development corporation resigned. An experienced SECO staff member was moved up to become director of both. A drive was launched to rejuvenate the organization by increasing participation and giving more attention to the needs of member groups. Pressure activities in support of member organizations became more frequent. Five hundred and fifty delegates took part in the April 19,

1980, Tenth Anniversary Congress and elected ten new, younger members to the eleven-person executive committee, including the first black person ever elected to the committee.

For a time, consideration was given to merging the executive committee of SECO and the board of the development corporation to unify planning and policy-making. However, it was decided that each decision group had an important job to do, that a little variety and competition were productive, and that the single executive director for both groups could provide coordination and unity.

In the course of this change, SECO became a general contractor. It came to own and operate an apartment complex of twenty-four units for senior citizens. It incorporated and currently runs a project for real estate brokerage, called Community Properties, Inc. It developed a joint-venture drugstore and has begun two housing syndications, low- to moderate-income developments.

In its twelve years of ups and downs as a coalition organization concerned with neighborhood improvement, SECO has tested many tactics and techniques. The organization had been underway for only two years when staff and volunteer leaders agreed on the need for self-assessment. A weekend retreat away from the neighborhood was used for serious discussion of accountability, decision-making, personnel policy, and simply "trusting." Some group dynamics techniques were utilized. Staff and volunteers participating became more acutely aware of the large commitment demanded of them. A few dropped out of the organization, feeling the commitment required was too great. It was then that the permanent, responsible organization with tough-minded leadership came into being.

From time to time SECO has had one-day or half-day training sessions for staff and volunteer leaders on such subjects as how to run a meeting. It has also used the longer, formal training programs of the National Center for Urban Ethnic Affairs.

An organizer for SECO must be an able recruiter and trainer of people, and must also become skilled in research and planning and gain some understanding of economics.

There has usually been some tension between the community organization staff working for SECO and the economic development staff of the corporation. The organization staff has tended to be concerned with the present, and with mobilizing people. The economic development staff has tended to be concerned with the future, and with mobilizing money and other resources. The single executive director holds joint staff meetings as a means toward coordination.

When it has faced a neighborhood issue, SECO has attempted to come up with an imaginative solution, "a better idea," that is positive. It also has sought to unite its member organizations into a relatively harmonious force which fights only with organizations outside the SECO coalition. An effort is made to avoid battles between groups within the coalition. SECO has also found that it must sometimes be ready to work with outside groups.

As a coalition, SECO has taken on only the large issues its member organizations cannot solve for themselves. When SECO does decide to move on an issue, it finds hitting the issue head-on pays off. No quiet behind-the-scenes maneuvering, whether the goal is reducing drug abuse among Southeast teen-agers, or stopping the state from anchoring a prison ship in its harbor.

As SECO takes on an issue it engages in a certain amount of fact-gathering and has found that careful research pays off. Sometimes this research is done by volunteers with little staff support, and sometimes primarily by staff. SECO has come to the conclusion that on technical matters, such as tax assessments, it must have a staff capability to do the special research required. University resources also have been tapped.

SECO has recruited volunteers by tackling specific issues: school desegregation, the expressway, housing improvement, tax assessments, and the like. Each issue attracts new people, some of whom become active members. SECO has always put its main emphasis not on winning battles but on finding able leaders who can think, decide, and move effectively.

SECO has learned from experience that it has to have accurate and frequent reports on what other groups in the neighborhood are doing, so that if their actions begin to run counter to SECO's objectives for the community, some quick action can be taken. It learned its lesson from a school desegregation coalition which handled desegregation effectively but bungled other education issues.

Over time SECO has learned the importance of maintaining amiable working relationships with all organizations within Southeast Baltimore. It became acutely aware of the importance of this when non-SECO groups in Southeast disagreed with the coalition over a new truck route, making it possible for city government to play one group against the other without taking any action to solve the problem.

The community constituency for social and human service delivery is much smaller than the constituency for issue pressure and housing and economic development. SECO is largely a community of extended families and strong church and fraternal organizations. There is a strong sense of privacy and self-reliance about family and social life. Organizing to obtain social service entitlements or rights has not been popular, making it hard to get people to come to meetings on social services. The organization has pushed ahead on services anyway because the leadership feels it is responsible for meeting real needs when government will not or cannot. But SECO has found that even most of the unemployed in its midst have too much pride to ask for assistance. They tend to tighten their belts and get what help they must have from within their own families.

A human services task force was organized in 1976 which carried out a four year neighborhood and family services demonstration project. The task force was a remarkable mixture of community leaders, natural helpers, former patients, and ordinary citizens concerned with mental health and family issues. Finding ways to work closely with professionals, the task force helped bring into being a hotline, referral directory, family day picnic for the neighborhood, a council of human service providers, a babysitting cooperative for young mothers, bus trips for the elderly and shut-ins, and a series of workshops on stress. The programs largely were built around networks of natural helpers discovered in the neighborhood.*

SECO has determined several criteria necessary before it will launch a new service program:

1. The new service should be developed by residents and fill a gap not being met by government or private agencies.
2. It should provide a combination of private and public resources and capabilities not available to a purely governmental operation or not normal in a private system.
3. It should use resources of the community which are generally not integrated into programs by traditional or governmental approaches.

* For more about this human service effort, see Arthur J. Naparstek, David E. Biegel, and Herzl R. Spiro, *Neighborhood Networks for Humane Mental Health Care* (New York: Plenum Press, 1982).

4. It should employ community residents in new roles that combine the best of professional skill and knowledge of the indigenous community and should enable them to gain skill in a manner not seen in traditional agencies or government programs.
5. Neighborhood people should be available to serve on a board for the service, which should be governed by community residents.
6. It should use a service delivery method that is adapted to the indigenous culture of Southeast Baltimore in a manner that would not be possible for a large agency with a metropolitan or statewide focus.

Money comes to SECO from a wide variety of sources, including United Way, the Ford Foundation, city government, corporations, private local foundations, and neighborhood people. Some funds have come from the supermarket it helped to sponsor. The organization feels it is safer to practice pressure activities when a cutoff of funds from one source would not be fatal. SECO would not like to become heavily dependent on city government or any other single source. Since most of its funds come from private sources, the Reagan cutbacks have not affected the organization's budget. SECO finished its 1982 fiscal year in the strongest financial position in twelve years. However, it was running into new difficulties obtaining funds for housing programs and new economic development projects. These programs were sure to be slowed down.

In 1982, SECO was pragmatic and hard-nosed. If a member organization wanted support on an issue, it had to be active in SECO, sending delegates to the congress and senate meetings. And the leadership was back to believing that to maintain SECO's influence and the respect of its funding sources, it had to maintain its ability "to put 400 people on the steps of city hall."

Western Addition Project Area Committee (San Francisco)

Citizen participation is old stuff to San Francisco. It was a peaceful little Hispanic-flavored town of eight hundred in 1848 when gold was discovered. The town exploded into a chaotic city of ten thousand in two years. Some citizens who were more interested in raising families and building businesses than in robbing drunks and strangling prostitutes came together to discuss their dangerous environment. They decided on a service strategy: they would form their own security force and dispense vigilante justice. For a short period, citizen power had a direct effect on the quality of the environment. The tradition of citizen power has persisted in this sparkling saltwater city, with its unusually diverse population groups.

Back in the 1960s the antipoverty program brought opportunities for less affluent people, especially blacks, to form cadres and bull their way into control of public decisions and money. In 1966 they fought Mayor John Shelley for weeks, demanding a majority of seats on the city's new antipoverty board, threatening demonstrations, and hinting at the possibility of violence. Newspaper attention helped build tension. Blacks, Hispanics, and others from minority neighborhoods argued that if the program was to be free of old-time politics and truly to counteract poverty, citizens had to run it. The mayor answered that his continued control would ensure liaison with public agencies and support from employers.

After forty-nine representatives from Spanish, black, Native American, Chinese, church, labor, political, and neighborhood organizations spoke for citizen control at a public hearing, the mayor capitulated. Citizens took control of a multimillion-dollar budget. Members of neighborhood antipoverty boards became neighborhood legislators. Their meetings became forums for citizen debate and decision-making. Their efforts appeared to be creating a new, unofficial arm of local government, one of persuasion and pressure.

Black citizens who became the top leaders of the San Francisco antipoverty program reasoned that while they had a few million to spend, the traditional urban institutions supplying education, welfare, health, housing, and the like had hundreds of millions. There was more to be gained, they felt, from advocacy than from building their own services. This meant that when they were not distracted by in-fighting, they spent their energies pushing large institutions to do more, spend more, for poor people. It was a pressure strategy, with a vengeance.

In the Western Addition neighborhood there was an all-out experiment. The neighborhood was divided into thirty-two small subneighborhoods, each of which elected a representative to a new Western Addition policy board whose members, amid wheeling and dealing suggestive of patronage politics, passed out jobs to friends and neighbors. Mountains of money were available. The new board hired 120 paid organizers, 50 full-time, 70 part-time, to organize an irresistible pressure group.

Each subneighborhood had a full-time organizer and two or three part-time people hired from the sub-neighborhood, one of whom was assigned to run a telephone chain.

Results from this pressure-power effort were slow in coming, and residents grew restless. One staff organizer reported, "People want more to eat and fewer meetings." The neighborhood office was picketed by residents who felt too much money had been spent on staff salaries and not enough on services. Federal officials who furnished the money echoed this complaint.

The main problem, however, was that masses of people were not mobilized to forge a lever strong enough to move the housing authority, welfare department, and other institutions. Those hired were not competent organizers.

People attending subneighborhood meetings, the heart of the effort, reported an average of thirteen present, and no sense of urgency among those attending. Serious issues were not aggressively addressed; a cohesive campaign did not come together. The staff organizers were not trained or led effectively. It was one of the great missed opportunities of neighborhood organizing. As one of the lead organizers pointed out, most of the paid staff were residents "doing the same thing they used to do as volunteers." There were not enough victories, not enough results to win people's confidence.

By late 1966 the large-scale pressure-power scheme was laid to rest. The neighborhood board shifted to a mixed strategy with emphasis on contracting with institutions for services that residents identified as being needed. However, although the great scheme did not work, a tradition of citizen control did become established in Western Addition.

Western Addition has had a sizable black population since World War II. It also has Asians and whites.

The neighborhood occupies a relatively flat slab of land just west of downtown. It is heavy on three-story structures, some of them elegant Victorian frame houses, some stucco, brick, and stone buildings. The street pattern is gridiron. There are long strip shopping streets and some cultural landmarks, like Bill Graham's deteriorating Winterland rock mecca and Jim Jones's ill-fated Peoples

Temple. Back in the 1950s and early 1960s some of the houses became overcrowded and shabby, not so much on the outside, where they were kept painted in white or pastel yellow and pinks, but on the inside where they were crowded and maintenance was neglected.

San Francisco was caught up in the fever of the Big Plan in those years. Dramatic redevelopment was launched downtown. Large new investments went into the festive Fisherman's Wharf, and planning began for the spectacular Bay Area Rapid Transit system and for drastic urban renewal in neighborhoods like Western Addition. Urban renewal was run by the Redevelopment Authority and involved big stakes: displacement of people and businesses, opportunities for jobs, investments, profits, and a modern environment. When they heard about it, the people of Western Addition wanted in on this government program.

By then it was 1968. Blacks in Western Addition had tasted a bit of power, and had a notion of what it meant to control public decision-making. An aggressive black pastor from the New Liberation United Presbyterian Church organized a coalition of organizations to resist some of the more drastic actions of the Redevelopment Authority. People lay down in front of bulldozers. Citizens went to court demanding control over the urban renewal program, claiming it was abusing the neighborhood without people being able to protect their rights. They pointed to the National Housing Act and other federal statutes, rules, and regulations that mandate citizen participation in local urban renewal programs. The U.S. District Court was sympathetic to the residents and ordered that an organization be established to provide residents with a voice in the project.

Out of this successful battle came the Western Addition Project Area Committee (WAPAC), a residents' organization charged with monitoring the urban renewal program, especially the relocation of residents and businesses, selection of developers, hiring practices of contractors, and rights of displaced people to be given priority for moving into new housing.

At first, the new organization tried operating with a big popular board of seventy-five, but it was difficult to achieve a quorum at most meetings. The board was cut to fifteen. Quorums then appeared regularly, since most of the fifteen were activists.

Board elections are promoted as a large public event. Here WAPAC uses an unusual technique. It hires an outside "election supervisor" to organize the elections. This increases objectivity in the management of the elections, and keeps a heavy workload off the backs of WAPAC's small staff. The supervisor might be a consultant, a team of knowledgeable people, or another organization. The San Francisco Redevelopment Authority, which pays WAPAC's bills, resents paying for an election supervisor, feeling WAPAC staff, board, and volunteers should organize the elections.

The election supervisor widely publicizes the coming election. Candidates file an application with the supervisor at least fourteen days before the election. Investigations are made to ensure a candidate's eligibility: he or she has to be a resident of Western Addition or belong to an organization with at least 90 percent of its membership living in the neighborhood.

Competition for board seats is strong. Candidates campaign for votes and urge people to come to the annual election meeting, where the voting takes place by secret ballot. Candidates have been known to hand out fried chicken in front of the election meeting place.

Turnouts have been as high as 1,000 and as low as 45, with 250 average. The annual election meeting has been used as a training school for residents, with workshops on such matters as housing speculation (how to keep down displacement), commercial development (how to get your own new business going in the neighborhood), and youth services (getting jobs for young people).

Nearly all board members have been black. The key board committee is planning and development. This small committee of five or six persons screens all proposals from would-be developers seeking to buy land cleared by the Redevelopment Authority. San Francisco is a booming city with a small land area. Cleared land close to downtown is scarce, and Western Addition land is much sought after. Prices are constantly rising. WAPAC's recommendations on land disposal carry great weight with the Redevelopment Authority.

An affirmative action committee monitors hiring related to urban renewal in Western Addition. It ensures that there is a strong minority hiring clause in all contracts for construction on cleared land. The committee also concerns itself with who works for the businesses and organizations occupying the new and remodeled buildings.

Although WAPAC has focused on its court-mandated participation and monitoring responsibilities, it has also acted on other neighborhood matters. It has sponsored an annual Juneteenth festival and a youth employment program in an area where jobs for young blacks have been scarce for decades. It successfully promoted a new

city recreation center, and new subsidized housing. It has been un-
successful in getting a new school.

Arnold Townsend, WAPAC's founding director, saw urban renewal as a process of removal. He also created a vision of what
Western Addition could be, a vision with emphasis on a strong social
fabric. Said Townsend:

> You have to have places for people to congregate and come together so
> they can begin to discuss like problems and begin to develop solutions to
> those problems, and if we don't never come together then you just have
> your own little house and you stay in there and you get in your own little
> car by yourself . . . and you keep yourself isolated and you never discuss
> nothing, and that's one of the major problems that's happening now.

In 1979, WAPAC's budget of $107,000 came from the Redevelop-
ment Authority. The budget had once been $170,000. The Authority
constantly chips away at the budget, claiming WAPAC has outlived
its usefulness and does not represent all the people of Western Addition, especially nonblacks.

In recent years there have been no funds for training. When funds
were more plentiful, there were annual board retreats where experts
helped board members understand the technical processes of urban
renewal, the many different government-aided housing programs,
and the affirmative action process, which is complicated legally.

The organization has no newsletter or newspaper of its own, but
it has made use of KPOO, the public radio station, where Townsend's voice became familiar to listeners. Much use has also been
made of the pages of two black newspapers, the *Courier* and the *Sun
Reporter*.

Protection of blacks' right to live in central San Francisco, with
some control over their own turf, has been the central driving issue
for WAPAC. Going into the 1980s, the most important aspect of that
issue became displacement caused by rising housing costs.

In late 1979 the *San Francisco Chronicle* reported resentment
toward gay investors moving into Western Addition, some of whom
were evicting black tenants. Blacks were angry. But at the same time
the paper said gay speculators were accusing black business people
of lacking the imagination to renovate Victorian buildings and to
make Western Addition's Fillmore Street shopping area a symbol of
cultural pride. WAPAC found blacks being forced to double up, two

families to a unit, or being driven across the bay to Oakland, where rents were a bit lower.

Part of the conflict has involved WAPAC's competition with another neighborhood organization in Western Addition which has some gay leadership, the Western Addition Neighborhood Association. The association is mainly white homeowners. It has raised questions about the fairness of WAPAC's system for granting priority certificates to people displaced by the urban renewal activity. It considers WAPAC to be a narrow, single-purpose agency, and not a real neighborhood organization dealing with all important community needs as they arise.

The rival association is a voluntary organization with no staff or office and a loose membership and fundraising policy. Anyone who comes to its public monthly meeting may vote. There are no dues, but the hat is passed at meetings to pay for mailings and refreshments. Forty to seventy people attend a meeting. It has a steering committee open to anyone, four officers, and no other structure.

Claiming a strong interest in preventing displacement, the association has sponsored forums on the city's heritage preservation low-interest loan program, through which low-income owners of old homes are helped to repair them. Their meetings have provided information on other programs for stabilizing rents, reducing housing speculation, and slowing the conversion of rental units to condominiums. The association encourages owners not to sell, and to build "sweat equity" by making their own improvements.

The association spent energy getting Bill Graham to close Winterland, which he did with a New Year's Eve concert featuring the Grateful Dead. Residents had long suffered from the restless antics of crowds of rock fans waiting to enter the popular old concert hall.

It has influence beyond its own numbers. Its expanded influence comes partly from its informal connections to the powerful San Francisco gay community, and partly from membership in the Coalition for San Francisco neighborhoods, an alliance of thirty-seven organizations, most from white middle-income neighborhoods. Through the Coalition the association joins in bimonthly meetings with the mayor, where neighborhood organizations set forth their concerns. WAPAC is not a member of the Coalition.

While the association expands its influence, WAPAC is having difficulty surviving. It has no independent source of funds, and its constituency is shrinking as the black population in Western Addition declines. The urban renewal project eventually will be closed out, and WAPAC's funds will disappear with it. This could leave the blacks remaining in Western Addition without a strong voice in neighborhood affairs.

In 1982, a new staff was moving in directions to give WAPAC renewed life. It was arguing that, since the San Francisco Housing Authority annually cited WAPAC as evidence that the city was meeting its commitment to low- and moderate-income families, thus enabling the city to receive federal Community Development Block Grant funds, the city had a need to continue WAPAC.

WAPAC was also moving to find new ways to act as advocate for the minority poor. City government is moving toward a policy of requiring developers of commercial space to contribute to a fund for low- and moderate-income housing. WAPAC is negotiating with downtown developers to apply such contributions to the Western Addition neighborhood.

WAPAC is also moving to help the neighborhood gain control of some of the cleared parcels in the commercial section of Fillmore Street with the possibility of some income flowing to WAPAC. The organization is negotiating agreements with Safeway to train low-income women to become checkers in a new facility on Fillmore, and to make space available in the shopping center for small businesses displaced by the renewal effort.

Another opportunity pursued involves the city's condominium policy. Condo developers are required either to set aside 20 percent of units for low-income residents or to make an equivalent investment in low-income housing off-site. WAPAC seeks to bring some of the investment into Western Addition.

The organization is establishing a new neighborhood development corporation which will seek to sponsor housing and economic development ventures, and utilize some of the initiatives mentioned earlier in ways that will ensure WAPAC continuity.

As its political base declines with loss in black population, WAPAC is becoming allied with low-income housing groups in other neighborhoods, including Hunters Point, Chinatown, and Mission, to find ways to avoid further displacement of low-income people.

If some of these new efforts take hold, WAPAC may yet survive.

Upper Albany Community Organization (Hartford)

Hartford, Connecticut, is a historic urban place, with beginnings in the Dutch fort "Good Hope" built in 1633. It was chartered as a city in 1784, and ten years later the first insurance policy was written there. Insurance has since become Hartford's leading industry, with forty companies headquartered in and around the city.

Hartford is the heart of a metropolitan area of 700,000 people, but only a fifth of them are residents of the city itself. More than half of the city's 140,000 people are black or Hispanic, and many are poor and unemployed. Unemployment has been rampant among minorities for years, and the Reagan recession has made it worse.

Several Hartford insurance companies, along with other corporations, have long had a concern for problems of the city and in recent years have supported the building of strong neighborhood organizations. They have done this both individually and collectively, through Greater Hartford Process, Inc., their civic arm, which has sought to bridge the gap between the city's prosperous white-collar population and its suffering unskilled poor population.

Corporate leaders seem fearful that poverty, unemployment, and the accompanying crime, drug addiction, and hopelessness will destroy the city's vital business environment. Through Process they aim to help "meet the economic and social needs of Hartford residents, with emphasis on those special needs of low and moderate income and minority citizens."*

With and without the assistance of Process and the corporations, Hartford residents have formed many neighborhood organizations. One of the most prominent is the Upper Albany Community Organization (UACO), which, like Southeast Community Organization of Baltimore, has faced pulling and hauling between pressure and service.

Upper Albany is a large neighborhood northeast of downtown. Its largely black population numbers about thirteen thousand. UACO began in 1972, and from its beginning has been black-run. It grew

---

* These quotes are from the 1978-79 *Planning Report of Greater Hartford Process Inc.*, produced under the leadership of Morton Coleman, then president of Greater Hartford Process. In 1983, Process was merged into the Greater Hartford Chamber of Commerce.

out of the community work of the Horace Bushnell Church, an important neighborhood institution. Back in 1972 the social action committee of the church sponsored an aggressive weekly tabloid, the *North Hartford Truth*, which sought to inform the community on issues such as overcharging by the telephone company, worsening housing conditions, and neighborhood unemployment. The editor was Leonard Sengali, the church's outreach minister, who served as UACO's board president in the late 1970s.

The early efforts of Sengali and his social action committee expanded from crusading and pressuring with a community newspaper to making needs surveys and then launching UACO as an organization of individual members. Many of the original board members were poor. To encourage participation, they were paid a stipend of $18 a month, which did seem to increase attendance.

With the aid of Greater Hartford Process, Inc., a grant was obtained from the Ford Foundation. Under the guidance of Process, UACO formulated a comprehensive services-development strategy calling for broad programs of housing construction and renovation, neighborhood economic development, and social services.

While the young organization continued to do some crusading on neighborhood issues, most of its efforts focused on planning a shopping center and on housing and social services. By 1975 there were few concrete results, and the organization began running out of money. The executive director left. The remaining staff, confident of UACO's future, teamed with Process to create a persuasive fundraising pitch, setting forth an exciting vision of a dynamic, expanded UACO. This was presented to corporations, city government, and the media. Corporate dollars and some of the city's community development block grant funds were committed to UACO.

Phillip Morrow, neighborhood coordinator at Process, had worked on the new financing package and became the new executive director. Morrow was an experienced organizer, who had put together the Poor People's Federation in Connecticut. Under his leadership the board was broadened to include people from outside the area, including representatives of surrounding neighborhoods. Money problems ended the board member stipends.

UACO then concentrated on major development projects, including the shopping center, a plant to manufacture solar energy hardware, and numerous renovated and new houses. Services created or expanded were recreation programs, a crisis intervention unit, youth counseling, a 24-hour information and referral hotline, and a community resource directory. Volunteers were recruited and trained to work with these services.

In 1978, HUD selected UACO as one of the nation's twenty-one "advanced neighborhood development organizations" and made a special grant to the organization. This helped push the UACO budget to a million dollars. Although a few thousand dollars came from five hundred dues-paying members, the bulk of the money was contributed by a dozen sources among governments, foundations, and corporations. UACO has been unusual in the extensive support it has obtained from profit-making corporations. Besides contributing funds, corporations have loaned specialists and technical experts to UACO. Staff have found most corporate people sympathetic and helpful to the organization, but from time to time they have felt that a corporate volunteer was unable to understand the special needs and difficulties of a nonprofit organization.

As the organization has moved forward to carry out its economic development projects, it has created subsidiary corporations to run them. Debate has gone on within UACO as to whether these should be made independent corporations with their own boards. Morrow felt these new corporations should be kept close to UACO, to ensure that they follow UACO policy, and feed their eventual profits back to UACO. He saw these profits as possible permanent funding for UACO. His view prevailed. The directors of the corporations were appointed from among the directors of UACO. However, no profits have ever flowed back, since there haven't been any.

UACO sought to work out relations with other organizations in the neighborhood. For example, it supported a local merchant association's efforts at store modernization and parking lot expansion.

A professional organizer from UACO, with a team of VISTA volunteers, helped build a strong network of block clubs and tenant associations which established its own storefront headquarters. UACO also sought to aid the clubs and associations in several ways. It brought clubs and associations together in leadership meetings to discuss and resolve community problems, and to take joint action on housing and street resurfacing. It helped them plan and carry out training programs for their members. Finally, UACO helped them deal with issues on individual blocks, including obtaining equipment for a neighborhood playground, raising money for fire victims, getting police to monitor speeding cars, planning with the city for capital improvements, and seeking funds for a senior citizen center.

The block clubs and tenant associations followed a militant pressure strategy and made strong demands upon city government on several neighborhood issues. UACO sought to stay in the background when these controversies erupted. The usual policy was to leave pressure to the block clubs. Occasionally, UACO formed a temporary coalition with organizations in the other four neighborhoods of north Hartford to press on some flagrant issue, but such pressure was exerted in the name of the coalition.

UACO leadership felt more could be done about the fundamental needs of jobs and housing if emphasis was on businesslike negotiation, enterprise, and professional services, rather then pushing and shouting. The businesslike approach could bring sizable government and corporate grants to a self-help black organization with plans and energy.

Philip Morrow consistently upheld the view that "UACO did not take public stands on divisive issues, but has and does speak loudly for the interests of neighborhood advancement, and improvement of the quality of life in Upper Albany. Any group would be pulled apart if they jump on every issue of controversy without first gaining a consensus of its constituents."

The block clubs asked UACO for board seats, and their representatives were appointed to fill half a dozen vacancies. These representatives pressed their fellow board members to give less attention to development and more to crime and other neighborhood issues bothering people in the blocks. The new representatives also seemed to resent development plans which they felt had been made without participation by the block clubs.

The technical and legal requirements of development always made UACO's program more remote from general community understanding than social service delivery or advocacy. The community began to miss the "hands-on," immediate quality of social services and advocacy as the development agenda increased. This became a source of contention within the board.

Meanwhile, UACO's burgeoning budget and ambitious programs generated more than power and opportunity. They created management problems common to most rapidly growing organizations. Files and records scattered among several expanding departments caused a need for central record-keeping, which is expensive. The numerous and varied funding sources freed the organization from dependence on a single source and enabled it to maintain its independence. But they also became a burden because of their varied requirements for financial records and reporting. UACO employed its own staff accountant to oversee and maintain the records. An insurance company, on occasion, loaned a financial expert to help solve difficult financial management problems.

Staff size brought other complications. Openings for jobs had to be advertised widely, including notification to block clubs and other community organizations. As usually happens, jockeying for staff positions created hostility.

There were a variety of training programs for staff. Promotion was generally from within, and staff members had benefits similar to those of corporate employees. Maintaining communications flow among all staff in a large expanding organization, with a complex, ever-changing program, was difficult. Each department sought to hold weekly staff meetings, with the full staff meeting every two weeks.

The staff and board recognized that their greatest need was to transform plans and grants into results—the always difficult problem of implementation. In UACO's 1979 annual report, President Sengali urged: "Here we are, a full-grown and yet still-fledgling organization, almost a prototype of the community that we represent. A first-class organization desperately attempting to stay afloat amidst predictions of failure. We have survived, but the future continues to pose a threat to us."

During 1978 and 1979 disagreements arose between the executive director and some board members over matters beyond block club participation and UACO involvement in neighborhood issues. These matters included the amount of financial information being supplied to the board, whether the board was being adequately consulted on hiring for senior staff positions, and the pace of program implementation. Such disagreements are common to large organizations with active boards and a strong executive director. The director finally moved to HUD to take an important post as head of the then new Office of Public-Private Partnerships.

At the beginning of the 1980s a new executive director stepped into this potentially important organization to face turmoil and growing pains. He was Ben Andrews, a state officer of the NAACP who had run for Congress. He was immediately sensitive to the need for UACO to be tied closely to neighborhood residents, as well as to the importance of speeding up the shopping center and housing developments.

Andrews has emphasized what he calls "re-merging" UACO's identity with that of the community. This means placing a greater emphasis on community organizing and social services, and also expanding coordinated efforts with the block clubs on specific issues. The block clubs strike out militantly against city government on an issue. The city agrees to do something. UACO moves in with professional and technical assistance to ensure that specific solutions are formulated and carried out, keeping the block clubs informed. The city respects both UACO's responsible way of doing business and the power of block residents linked to it.

An example concerns police protection. Instead of complaining about protection in the community, UACO helped the block clubs raise the issue. The city responded to the demands coming from the clubs while UACO stayed out of the fray and preserved its technical character.

UACO is now consulting the block clubs about allocation of program money, seeking their advice, and reporting back to them regularly. It is assisting the block clubs to make the voice of the community more widely heard. Residents appear to be increasing their influence within the organization, and, through their block clubs, to be enlarging their influence in the city.

Ultimately, UACO's ability to hold and expand the support of residents, corporations, and government depends on its ability to make good on its imaginative development plans. In housing development, UACO has made important gains over the past three years. It has sold twenty-seven units of two- and three- family residences which it rehabilitated with its own construction crews. It has developed seventeen low-cost condominiums, with outside contractors. It also has developed twelve units which it owns and manages. It is breaking ground for six new units and packaging another twenty-four units for development. Andrews projects a target of one hundred units owned and managed by UACO over the next few years, financed by a combination of public and private sources. The organization hopes that the ownership and management of these units, as well as development fees, will provide income to help support UACO administrative operations.

On the service side, UACO has state contracts for mental health, handicapped services, and crisis intervention. It is contemplating more local social service contracts. In 1982, it received a multiyear commitment of money from a large insurance company in Hartford.

Ben Andrews feels that neighborhood development organizations are in a period of transition. The groups that will make it through this transition are those with a strong mix of development and service contracts from local and state sources. He believes that strong block organizing is the lever to achieve a greater share of service contracts. However, as this happens, UACO strategy will have to be restructured to absorb community accountability pressures. Just as block club pressure drives the city to hire UACO to furnish services, it can also put UACO under pressure to produce.

Focus on Renewal Neighborhood Corporation (McKees Rocks, Pa.)

McKees Rocks and Stowe Township are two bleak old factory towns forming an industrial community near the Ohio River on the western edge of Pittsburgh. There are twenty thousand people and eighty-three taverns. Peopled by hard-working folk, mostly Slavic and Italian in background, they are governed by plodding, neglectful, sometimes inept public officials. For several years the officials have been needled and pushed by the staff and members of the Focus on Renewal Neighborhood Corporation, an organization which has boldly sought to combine pressure and services in a flamboyant mixed strategy.

Focus on Renewal (FOR) was begun with the support of the Catholic diocese in 1969. Through this lively organization hundreds of citizens have worked to provide many needed services for the community, and to pressure public officials concerning garbage, schools, and rub-parlors. FOR grew out of a militant citizens committee headed by an optometrist and a priest which had formed in 1965 to fight successfully for an antipoverty program for the area. The then dominant local politician had opposed the program because he feared he could not control it.

Early on, FOR divided McKees Rocks and Stowe Township into twenty-one little neighborhoods and attempted to have a small suborganization in each. Formally, the twenty-one subgroups make up the neighborhood corporation. The twenty-one presidents are the board of the corporation.

From time to time a subneighborhood group may meet, but the principal citizen involvement is built around an occasional town meeting in which people from all twenty-one little neighborhoods meet en masse. One hundred people are required for a quorum at a town meeting. Theoretically, it is here that the large decisions of the corporation are debated and decided, with every member present having a vote. Leaders of FOR insist that the assembly form of decision-making is the essential method upon which the corporation must be built. It is a bedrock principle of FOR that every citizen have a "legislative vote" in policy-making. But as the years go by, the organization finds it increasingly difficult to keep this principle working.

FOR operates a number of services, each with its own board. It owns a building on a main street where most of its activities are centered. It is an old bank building, handsomely remodeled by volunteers.

The staff of FOR includes twenty-two full-time and twelve part-time employees. The greatest part of this staff works on health services, under a direct federal grant from the Urban Health Initiatives program of the National Institutes of Health. That program provides $180,000 a year for a staff of three physicians and a dentist, with a complement of specialists, interns, nurses, and other personnel to handle 24,000 medical and dental encounters a year, including service to several hundred homebound seniors. Medical and dental services are provided on a sliding-scale fee basis.

FOR also serves forty lunches a day to senior citizens, with a large array of senior programs. Its food cooperative purchases $40,000 in produce a year. The FOR credit union has $200,000 in assets and lends to a maximum of $5,000.

The leadership of the corporation has been in the hands of staff. The staff director is a Catholic priest, and the associate director a nun. They give all of their waking time to the affairs of the corporation. The president of the corporation has been a staff employee working under them. The leadership team of director and associate director are dedicated, persistent, and aggressive. They tend to dominate not only the corporation but the headlines it receives, which are numerous.

Many citizens have subroles of leadership in the corporation, serving on one of the separate boards for each service, or on the corporation board. The by-laws require a year's service before a person can become an officer.

The staff feel they must take public positions on issues because as crises occur and events unfold there is not always time for the corporate assembly to meet and decide. Staff members distinguish between a staff position on an issue and a corporate position. Staff positions are taken much more often than corporate positions. The staff have found that volunteers in the organization are often intimidated by local politicians, and cannot be depended upon in confrontations at public hearings and elsewhere. Hence, staff often appear alone as advocates before public bodies.

The director and associate director serve as organizers for the corporation, as well as administrators for the staff who provide services. In the past, the staff has occasionally organized a weekend of training for a group of citizens. Held in a lodge or institution, the training has covered philosophy, issues, and techniques. When staff members attend an out-of-town conference, several citizens are taken along. Otherwise, there is no formal recruitment and training process for volunteer leadership.

In addition to serving important needs, the leadership considers the services as essential to recruiting volunteers for the corporation. They feel the services give the corporation legitimacy in the eyes of the general community. Something worthwhile is visible to all citizens.

On the pressure front, FOR is constantly pressing the Stowe and McKees Rocks governing councils, and the joint school board, on issues involving more say for citizens in budget-making, uses of community development funds, building of a new high school, and the like. It has also fought the county board over the issue of removing human services from the neighborhood.

Many neighborhood organizations consider simultaneous involvement in service delivery and pressure a highly risky business, with one apt to get in the way of the other. FOR believes they fit together, with services producing the people-power for strong pressure positions. Fear of combining the two is usually based on concern that advocacy positions will cause loss of funding for services. FOR has lost funding, but it refuses to back down from its advocacy position. This is a matter of justice and principle with FOR. FOR describes its program:

> The neighborhood corporation . . . has always stood firmly on the
> building blocks of human services for the needy and resistance to the in-
> justices which have kept our people in that position of need. Over the
> years we have made many friends in providing the services; over the
> years we have made many enemies in announcing the injustices [they
> suffer].

A goal sought since 1974 is to give Stowe Township and McKees
Rocks assembly government. In assembly government, direct legislative power for the municipality is placed in a town meeting of
registered voters. To this end FOR has sought to elect sympathetic
government study commissions which would be empowered to write
new charters for the two municipalities. The proposed charters
would provide for assembly government, and be presented to the
voters for approval.

In May 1981 the voters of McKees Rocks elected a charter commission slate that was organized by FOR. The commission proposed
a new charter with a town meeting government which would have
no elected officials. The only executive officer would be a town
manager appointed by the direct assembly. The commission feared
that elected officials would put the politicians back in power. From
their independently elected position, they might subordinate the
assembly power.

The new charter was on the November 1982 ballot. The politicians in power attacked it as likely to bring "mob rule" and "higher
taxes." There was also a whispering campaign among white voters
warning "blacks from the projects will pack the town meetings and
run the town." The charter proposal was defeated 1,660 to 993. FOR
leadership is undaunted, determined to keep at it until it finally persuades a majority to try assembly government.

The mixed strategy of pressure politics and service delivery has
been costly to FOR. A grant for $70,000 a year for the senior
citizens program was once cut off and awarded to a Catholic church
elsewhere in the area where some of the local politicians, at odds
with FOR, are members.

County government, in cutting off the funds, alleged it had received complaints about service at the FOR center, and that the
center staff had refused to open all their records. Staff of FOR said
the cutoff came because FOR raised questions about centralization
of nutrition, health, and transportation services away from the

neighborhoods. They also alleged that cutoff was punishment because they had offended local politicians who carry weight in county government.

The mainstay of public resources for FOR comes from a direct categorical federal program which is relatively immune to local political pressures. Small-town politicians from McKees Rocks and Stowe did not have the power to derail this federal support. And FOR does have the scope of activity to impress federal health officials with its productivity.

FOR has plunged ahead with its own fundraising. It continually seeks contributions and foundation and federal grants. FOR feels it will be much stronger if it can raise many hundreds of dollars every week from individual contributors. After losing its grant, FOR kept its senior citizens center operating at almost full program. At the same time the FOR staff went to the Department of Health and Human Services in Washington seeking funds for a family health center. Eventually, $195,000 was obtained for medical supplies, equipment, and staff. In addition, the National Health Service Corps furnished a full-time pediatrician, nurse-practitioner, dentist, nutritionist, and hygienist. This is the basis of its present health and social services program.

FOR receives a basic operating grant of about $20,000 from the Catholic diocese. An important point can be made about diocesan support. It has been steady and has anchored FOR on a minimal but still solid ground of support. When grants and contracts are cut off for political reasons, the organization turns to its survival mode based on diocesan support, low-paid clergy staff, and volunteers to hang on until new service dollars can be found. When they are found, the organization returns to a full-staff model.

The leadership of FOR is acutely aware of the importance of citizen control. They want it for their community but have been frustrated in many of their attempts. They see their source of power being the active support of large numbers of ordinary residents who are attracted to FOR by having their self-interest served through one or more of the FOR services. But citizen control of FOR itself is limited. This is the way it would survive if hit by heavy federal cuts in funds, but this has not yet happened. Rather than retrench, FOR was planning to open a second building in 1983.

Sometimes through picketing, packing town council meetings, and sponsoring other demonstrations, FOR has attempted to show its power, but it is mostly staff that has been visible. Its senior citizen members write letters and telephone, but there is little out-front display of strong leadership by volunteers. The leadership roles remain largely with staff. People outside FOR have become aware of this, and it weakens the organization in their eyes.

FOR was founded as a church-supported community organization. The priest and nun who founded the organization, their successors, and those immediately around them have had a definitive view of FOR as a religiously motivated community organization. From its inception, FOR has rested upon a theologically informed method of organizing. FOR's theory of community organization and organizing place a premium on religiously oriented leadership. Leadership by the clergy staff in FOR is not a contradiction to citizen control, but a model for citizen control, in the eyes of that staff.

FOR has no regular research program. It does research issue by issue on an ad hoc basis. Sometimes people at one of the universities aid a research effort. FOR staff members have become adept at obtaining needed information from government offices.

FOR publishes a monthly newspaper, which is sent to all five thousand households listed on the voter registration roles for Stowe and McKees Rocks. It uses this newspaper to inform the public about the services available, and about issues of injustice with which FOR is involved. The paper openly pressures government, slaps enemies, and appreciates friends.

From long experience FOR has come to distrust most government officials, and especially those in local town government whom FOR has monitored for years. FOR leaders are convinced that many local officials are not only incompetent and insensitive to people's needs, but also corrupt. This view has inspired FOR's eight-year battle for direct assembly government.

FOR leadership speaks up often at meetings of the school board and town councils, but these governmental bodies resist listening to them. Sometimes a meeting will be adjourned or the plug pulled on the public address system when an FOR leader speaks. Sister Paulett, the former associate director, was arrested several times.

During 1979 and 1980 FOR fought a running battle with the McKees Rocks borough government over attempts by the borough to borrow money to pay debts. FOR accused the borough of seeking an illegal loan and of sleazy financial operations which deprived the community of needed public services and improvements. FOR also charged that citizens were not given adequate opportunity to participate in spending decisions. FOR went into court to try to stop the borrowing and persuaded the judge to cut the amount from $165,000 to $65,000. FOR also filed charges with the state government. Receiving government grants has not diminished FOR's militant pressure efforts on behalf of what it believes to be justice.

FOR has a rather elaborate formal structure on paper, but informally it is largely staff-led, and much of the twenty-one-neighborhoods structure seems to be dormant. The attempt to use an assembly to govern FOR is impressive, but upon attending a FOR assembly one finds the agenda is mainly reports and announcements which require no debate or decision and that staff rather than citizens are in control.

The services provided by FOR are first-rate, in both their quantity and their quality. They are vital in the relatively deprived community of McKees Rocks and Stowe Township. For some people they are the only services they can afford. FOR has reached thousands of people in one way or another, and continually expands to reach more. It may yet reach its goal of neighborhood people controlling the local government.

Neighborhood Housing Services, Inc., and
West Side Community Council (Salt Lake City)

In Salt Lake City, where self-reliance is a value long honored by practice, neighborhood organization has rolled on, even showing growth in the teeth of federal cutbacks. Values such as self-reliance flow from the extraordinary influence of religion on the city's life. In 1847 Prophet Brigham Young and a wagon train of determined brethren of the persecuted Church of Jesus Christ of Latter-Day Saints moved west in search of a place to settle in peace. About four hundred miles west of Denver these zealot pioneers climbed over the Wasatch Mountains and beheld a long river valley so fertile it seemed to fulfill the promise of the Book of Mormon: "and inasmuch as ye shall keep my commandments, ye shall prosper and shall be led to a land of promise; yea, even a land which I have prepared for you; yea, a land which is choice above all other lands" (I Nephi 2:20).

Settling in the valley below snow-capped peaks, they called in other members of the church, concentrated upon being devout and productive, and gradually created what is now the most important metropolis between Denver and San Francisco. It is a city where the dominant building in the skyline is world headquarters of the Mormons, and the largest department store and most elegant hotel are church-owned.

Salt Lake City's politics, laws, business, and neighborhoods are dominated by Mormon values: hard work, self-determination, and strong family life. Mormon families relate to the "ward," a small neighborhood church community with its own chapel building as center for social and spiritual life. Mormons form thick social networks in each neighborhood, with warm relationships.

Organizing to preserve and improve neighborhoods comes naturally to the residents of Salt Lake City. The notion that neighborhood people take responsibility for their own local community is strongly supported by Mormon values. Being fiercely independent and self-reliant, neighborhood people want no control from downtown agencies, although many are now willing to accept aids and support.

Neighborhood organization is entrenched in Salt Lake City. It influences government, and at the same time it is helped and co-opted by government. The city is officially divided into seven large communities. Organizations exist in each community and are given help and technical assistance (but no funds) by the city Department of Citizen Participation. This city department was formed in January 1979 as a response to mounting citizen demand for some say over the programs of city government.

Moving citizen participation into the established bureaucratic fold caused consternation among neighborhood leaders in Salt Lake City, according to Florence Bittner, who had been president of the Salt Lake Association of Community Councils, and became the city's first director for the Department of Citizen Participation. Florence Bittner believes:

> Always there is the need to walk a fine line [doing] active advocacy for neighborhoods without totally alienating the bureaucracy. Because of the political clout developed at the neighborhood level, the City has in most instances been responsive to neighborhood needs.

Her department provides neighborhood organizations with minimal services such as mailings, secretarial help, telephoning, and complaint resolution. It has become the city's office for receiving citizen complaints, and has taken on a neighborhood-related anticrime program begun with Law Enforcement Assistance Act (LEAA) funds.

Some neighborhood leaders in Salt Lake City feel that a neighborhood organization could become dependent on the department's services and lose its ability to make free decisions, especially when differences with city government might be involved. To date, however, differences have been few. The Mormon environment helps achieve a formal harmony.

Probably the fastest-growing and most innovative neighborhood organization is Neighborhood Housing Services, headed by able, quietly aggressive David Nimkin. Salt Lake's Neighborhood Housing Services (NHS) is one of 150 similarly named housing improvement organizations spread across the nation, all modeled after a pioneering effort by residents of a Pittsburgh neighborhood begun in the late 1960s. The chief characteristic of NHS is partnership of lenders and government officials with residents.

Sale Lake City's NHS was begun in 1978 in Central City, oldest of the seven communities into which Salt Lake City divides. It is where the Mormon pioneers and their prosperous descendants built attractive gabled frame houses once they had moved beyond log cabins. Within this old and diverse community, there is a small neighborhood of twelve hundred homes around Liberty Park. This is where NHS began its operations. With its emphasis on local control and "neighbors helping neighbors," NHS has fit well in Salt Lake City.

When NHS began in 1978 there was some opposition from ultra-conservative Mormons who feared the program would lead to mandatory code enforcement and manipulation of helpless homeowners. These critics saw NHS as a "conspiracy by bankers" to make money from "forced" home improvement loans. Over time they have come to accept NHS.

Owners of 515 homes around the park have been assisted to improve their houses, and hundreds more have participated in other NHS-led neighborhood efforts. A stronger zoning law to protect the residential character was obtained, curbs were repaired, and a new mini-park was created in a corner of the area.

NHS has gone on to serve the nearby West Side. With its strong base of support from lending institutions and city government, it has flourished in the face of Reagonomics, although some of its support from savings and loan associations has declined as these associations have suffered severely from the recession and high interest rates.

NHS is governed by a board of seventeen: ten local residents, four lenders, two city officials, and one person from a corporation. They are elected by the three-hundred members of NHS, who meet once a year. Membership is free and open to all residents of the areas served.

The board hires the staff director, who in turn hires the other eight staff members. It sets policy at its monthly meetings. Operating funds for NHS have come largely from participating local financial institutions with Community Development money used for the low-interest NHS revolving loan fund. There have been some grant funds from foundations and government, and these are now on the increase. In five years the revolving loan fund, which makes loans to those who cannot secure them elsewhere, has grown from $100,000 to $600,000.

The annual operating budget has risen from $60,000 the first year to $182,000 for 1982-83. Services to residents include financial counseling, technical advice, help in obtaining bids from licensed contractors, monitoring remodeling jobs in progress, guidance on do-it-yourself projects, training workshops, energy audits, passive solar installations, and voluntary code inspections done with city cooperation.

With help from volunteers, NHS publishes a printed newsletter containing home improvement information, interviews with home-owners making improvements, profiles of newcomers, news of block club activities, details on services available, and related matters. It is published six times a year.

NHS sponsors an annual fair in its original neighborhood, which is now called East Liberty Park. The fair draws more than a thousand people and helps to build social fabric.

Volunteers are recruited by NHS to help elderly and handicapped homeowners make repairs. Some members of tough youth gangs have become volunteers.

Minority youth, including blacks and Hispanics, have become visible in recent years, generating neighborhood turmoil. NHS has involved them in projects to clean up vacant lots and replace expressway overpass graffiti with murals. It has organized a program in which weatherization companies hire and train youth.

Board and staff emphasize the Mormon tradition of neighbor help-ing neighbor. They feel this helps build trust among people, thereby advancing community solidarity and stability.

David Nimkin says NHS is working with a third generation of volunteers. The first generation were the determined people who founded NHS and served as its original board members. Some of these burned out along the way and receded into the background. Second-generation volunteers were homeowners principally inter-ested in protecting the single-family character of their neighbor-hood. These came together with NHS help and collectively pressed to have the area downzoned to stop apartment construction. Their goal achieved, most of these second-generation folk sat back. Now a third generation is at work made up of people taking out improve-ment loans through NHS, borrowing tools, and taking responsibility on committees or as leaders of affiliated block clubs.

In 1978, the staff and a board committee undertook organizing ef-forts not always associated with an NHS. The East Liberty Park neighborhood was divided into four parts, with a "quadrant" leader recruited for each. Quadrant leaders helped organize block clubs throughout their quadrants. The staff felt that by getting people to-gether they were helping form the skeleton of a full-scale organiza-tion, but that eventually the people would have to take over and go it on their own. This transition was taking place in 1982.

As block and quadrant leaders have solidified their own indepen-dent organization, NHS has been able to apply its energies to extend-ing its territory into the adjacent West Side Community.

The West Side is a large area—6.5 square miles with eight thou-sand households living mostly in single-family houses. There are some well-off families and a diverse mixture of minorities including Hispanics, blacks, Tongans, and Southeast Asian refugees. How-ever, the largest number are white middle-income folk living in modest but comfortable homes.

Sporadic organization activities began here in the 1940s, and by 1957 the West Side Community Council was in being. It consisted of a few residents concerned with housing conditions and public im-provements. They worked on a small scale until the 1960s, when a Model Cities program was established which provided funding for staff and office.

West Side Community Council has about thirty active members who keep it rolling. Until the sword of Reagonomics cut its wide swath in 1982, the organization had funds from the Salt Lake Community Action Program to pay for a small staff. With CAP funds gone, the council carries on with volunteers; even the former staff members are active.

Problems of concern to the council have been housing maintenance, parks and swimming pools, street conditions, and public education. As a CAP organization the council was once concerned with CAP services, including those for health care, child abuse and neglect, food stamps, protection against burglary, and the like.

The board of the council has twenty-four members who serve three-year terms, some members' terms expiring each year. A board member is limited to two three-year terms. To be a candidate requires residency and a petition of thirty signatures. Sometimes there are three or four candidates for each board seat. There are two polling places, with about a hundred and fifty residents voting. The board meets monthly, and any resident may attend and bring up an issue.

Board members actively recruit candidates among church members, and from PTAs and little leagues. There are committees for physical environment, education, social services, housing, and crime prevention, which hold short meetings on the same evening as the monthly board meeting, starting only about half an hour before the board meeting. Committees have four or five members each, some of whom are not board members.

Very important to the council's influence are its affiliations with the city's Department of Citizen Participation and the Salt Lake Association of Community Councils, a citywide nongovernmental coalition of community councils which has considerable respect and clout. Support from the association is useful to the West Side Council when it deals with the city or other established institution on some large issue.

Leaders of the council feel their growing influence is shown by the increased numbers of people who seek out the council for help with their problems, the real estate developers who come asking for support of a zoning change, and the willingness of NHS to extend its services into the community.

Mormons value authority highly. The West Side Community Council follows a cooperative approach in its dealings; its leaders believe confrontation only builds barriers. The council does use pressure, but in a mild form.

Research efforts of the council are on the usual ad hoc, as-needed basis. Aid on research has been provided by the city's Department of Planning and Zoning, particularly concerning a complex annexation of nearby county land. Council leadership has a positive attitude toward research. The council has sponsored a sample survey to learn about residents' needs, attitudes, and future plans. From CAP the council picked up the habit of annual evaluations.

With its loss of CAP funds, the council lost its newsletter, but this gap is being filled in part by the NHS newsletter. A commercial weekly newspaper serving the West Side, the *Sunset News,* readily carries news releases from both the council and NHS.

During most of its years the council had little direct contact with local business people, but it has recently moved to gain such involvement. NHS's partnership orientation is accelerating the participation of business people.

For a long time, the mayor and city council members have come to each of the city's seven communities, including the West Side, for an annual public forum where they listen to any and every complaint and request. A hundred people might show up, with twenty-five of them going to the microphone to complain about a dangerous railway crossing, a noisy moto-cross raceway, or the admission charge at a new swimming pool equipped with a wave-creating mechanism. Elected officials patiently seek to answer questions and comment on each complaint. Four of the city's seven city council members were once officers of community councils. Grant Maybe, city council member from the West Side, is a former vice-president of the West Side council. Generally, city council and the mayor are strongly supportive of neighborhoods. Even as Community Development Block Grant funds have declined, city council has sought to maintain the funds going to the neighborhoods.

L. Wayne Horrocks, who chaired the West Side Council during 1974-79 and is still active in its affairs, says the council helped change the West Side from "an ignored, step-child area" to a neighborhood in the midst of a $50 million public improvement effort. Additions underway include new curbs and gutters, small parks, a swimming pool, repaved and enlarged streets, a new railroad overpass, three bridges over the Jordan River, a parking lot for the senior citizens center, and additional roads for the local industrial park which Horrocks hopes will help generate new jobs for the neighborhood.

However, the West Side Council itself has had fairly low visibility. Now comes NHS, with a vigorous staff and dramatic program. Although NHS is making every effort to work through and with the West Side Council and its members, its high visibility is likely to overshadow the old council even as it puts some new life into it.

NHS has purchased and renovated an old building on the West Side for its new headquarters. It has its volunteer and jobs program with minority youth. With its enlarged loan fund it is helping owners of old houses to improve and brighten them. It is assisting a dozen young families to build their own new homes at a 50 percent saving.

In Salt Lake City, with a long tradition of self-help, the nation's new emphasis on local responsibility fits fine. The loss of federal funds has been little felt, so far.

Comment

Recession and federal cutbacks are slowing these organizations, but none is in danger of being killed off except perhaps the Western Addition Project Area Committee, which was brought into existence by court order to do a particular short-range task, and has not yet developed its own funding sources. Even WAPAC, as one of the few black neighborhood organizations in San Francisco concerned with low-income housing, might find a way to survive. The recession probably provides the opportunity for these service-development organizations to make a more credible case for grants and contributions, since hard times increase the need for their services. The notion that any of these organizations could become self-sufficient through their own enterprises seems, so far, to be a mirage. The need for subsidy seems to be long-term.

In most of the cases in this chapter, a neighborhood organization began as a group of people using pressure to gain something for their neighborhood. But somehow each of these neighborhood organizations found opportunities to obtain large grants to undertake what they felt were needed service or development programs. This changed each organization from one engaged primarily in political operations to one engaged primarily in administration. But in no case has the new situation been entirely satisfactory. Issues continually arise that services cannot solve. Residents of the local neighborhood communities periodically demand that their organizations act politically.

Each organization has found its own solution to this need to maintain a mixed strategy. SECO of Baltimore has reestablished outreach efforts to its small organization members and gives attention to their demands for support on crucial issues. UACO of Hartford has strengthened its ties to block clubs and aided them as they go out front to press on issues. FOR, of McKees Rocks, Pennsylvania, from the beginning of its service programs has not ceased to use pressure. It has paid a price but moved noisily on, shrilly having its say and pressing the issues. WAPAC of San Francisco, through its staff and board leadership, has continually pressed on urban renewal issues like public housing and unemployment. In Salt Lake City polite pressure on city hall has never let up.

Events and community demands exert pulls that must be responded to if a service organization is to retain its credibility in a neighborhood. Failure to respond could increase the chances for formation of a rival organization. Hence the tendency toward the mixed strategy.

All of the organizations have needed more active members, whether individuals or other organizations. Yet they seem disinclined to use their strongest lever to gain them: they give away their services without requiring active membership in return. Incentives are essential to getting members and keeping them active. A benefit offered can be a strong incentive. Health services, social services, jobs, training, housing, and the like offered by the organizations could be exchanged for joining the organization and giving active service to it. The organizations appear to be squeamish about adopting such a policy.

All of the organizations in this chapter draw large sums of money from one or more sources outside the neighborhood. They are thereby vulnerable. The money can give out, or be cut off. SECO and UACO have wisely sought to protect themselves by obtaining grants from many sources. If one grant is cut off, many others remain. NHS of Salt Lake City gains this protection by receiving funds from a variety of lenders and government sources.

WAPAC is weak, with all of its funds coming from one source, and even that arrangement is a temporary one. WAPAC seems only recently to have moved to diversify its sources.

FOR has the advantage of a semipermanent financial commitment from the Catholic diocese. Churches are communal rather than economic or government organizations. They are less likely to find their interests threatened by the actions of a confrontational group like FOR. Churches are people-based organizations. Most of their money comes from many small givers. They are free to take some risks on where to "invest." The self-interest of churches is served by neighborhood organizations since such organizations seek to preserve and improve the environment in which local churches exist. Churches are an appropriate, no-strings-attached money source for neighborhood organizations, but they do not seem to have as much to give away in the 1980s as they had in the 1970s.

Neighborhood organizations dependent on outside funding sources will always be subject to an uncertainty. This uncertainty is avoided by organizations that raise their own funds within their own neighborhood and survive on small budgets, as we saw in the last chapter.

UACO is the one organization that has been successful in obtaining support from corporations. NHS in Salt Lake, like NHS's elsewhere, has funds from lenders, but these are generally given under pressure of the Community Reinvestment Act. They decline when lenders are in financial trouble.

Corporations, other than lenders, give to UACO for a variety of reasons. Corporations in Hartford want stability in their city. They believe in the self-help ideal and want to encourage it. They feel the public relations from such giving will be favorable, and will thereby win good will for their products. Corporations everywhere probably will listen to such arguments, and many find them tempting.

SECO, FOR, and NHS publish informative printed newspapers which help strengthen their organizations. These publications attract users for services, build support for issues, strengthen social fabric, reward friends, and can punish enemies—although there is some hesitancy to use them for such a purpose. UACO has a periodic little newsletter. WAPAC is without a publication of its own. With their sizable budgets, it is difficult to understand why these organizations lack newspapers. As we saw in the last chapter, organizations in Wichita and Albuquerque with no staffs and tiny budgets publish effective newsletters which go to nearly every household in their neighborhoods.

SECO, UACO, and FOR each has a problem in its dealings with subgroups. The small neighborhood organizations affiliated with SECO do not always respond to calls for cooperation and support, or they make unreasonable demands for help. UACO is pressed by block clubs to play an advocacy role it does not wish to play. FOR on paper has twenty-one subneighborhood groups which are the base of the organization, but they do not really function.

These linked, decentralized suborganizations are essential to an organization's ties to the community. They are a major vehicle of participation. Without them the organization is weak, lacking a firm base. This weakness is to be noted particularly in the WAPAC organization. NHS in Salt Lake has a growing network of block clubs organized through NHS's own leadership. Up to now, this network has been a great source of strength to NHS, because the relationship is close and so far NHS and the block clubs have been in harmony on actions to be taken. There could come a day when NHS of Salt Lake would become subject to the same discomfort as UACO, with block clubs pressing for an advocacy position it does not wish to take.

All five organizations have an ever increasing need for influence and power. One route to power is coalition, joining up with organizations in other parts of the city or county to act jointly on issues, fund requests, and the like. SECO is large and covers a vast territory. It seems to feel it can operate without allies outside its own territory. UACO does coalesce with other organizations on the north side of Hartford, and gains from this. FOR eschews all alliances and probably has suffered, especially in dealing with county government. NHS in Salt Lake is working closely with the venerable West Side Community Council.

WAPAC has suffered in the past from a lack of essential alliances but is now moving to remedy this. It competes rather than cooperates with the other neighborhood organization in its area, although each has its own focus and constituency while sharing certain general objectives for neighborhood improvement. WAPAC stays out of the Coalition for San Francisco Neighborhoods although this citywide coalition might be able to help WAPAC maintain its funding. However, it is working with other low-income minority neighborhoods.

All of these big-budget organizations tend to have staff as spokespeople, rather than volunteer leaders. This is especially noticeable in FOR. FOR staff justify this practice by making a distinction between "staff" and "organization" positions on issues. However, it is doubtful that the public is able to make such a distinction, so in the public mind the staff becomes synonymous with FOR and its democratic, participative image is blurred. This public view is reinforced when FOR staff members sometimes serve as officers of the organization. Volunteer officers make any neighborhood organization more democratic and help to generate confidence within the community. FOR has experienced considerable hostility from some officials and citizens and could use an improved public image.

FOR staff claims that local politicians tend to intimidate citizens, so that it is best that staff take the heat and be out front in public hearings and confrontations. This policy has a high cost in loss of citizen growth and development, since much can be learned through the hard knocks of battle. The organization is wise in its insistence that full-time employees operating services be local residents. It would be consistent if the two top administrators, who come from the outside, would train local residents to assume some of their authority. The climate of the Sto-Rox community is provincial, and home-grown executives probably would command wider allegiance.

As an organization that seeks to follow the assembly method and achieve wide participation, it seems strange that FOR has no regular formal training program where members could learn the skills of negotiating, testifying, running meetings, making reports, writing proposals, and the like. The skilled administrators would seem capable of doing such training, and they certainly have access to training experts in other institutions, including church denominations and universities.

In Hartford, where block clubs are the principal vehicle for participation by neighborhood people, these clubs have not had a direct role in running UACO. UACO's thirty-person board and top staff have been the decision makers. Dues-paying members of UACO do elect the board, but a sizable number of members have always come from outside the neighborhood. UACO dues are low, so that presumably block club and tenant association members could dominate if they chose to join in large numbers. As pointed out, some block club members have been elected to the board but they do not control it.

FOR is building-centered: all its services are offered in one place, much like a traditional settlement house. The other organizations tend to have small offices, and spread out their service delivery stations. FOR owns its large building, which gives it the advantage of high visibility and stability. It also gives FOR the image of an establishment. The burden of maintaining buildings in good repair with all bills paid is a large one that takes energies that otherwise might be spent on program and advocacy.

Probably all of the organizations could benefit from expanded research programs. Among them, these organizations become involved in many complicated issues such as school construction, flood control, expressway routes, redevelopment financing, quality control of housing, rehabilitation, shopping center financing, integration, and the like. Knowing more about these complex issues, organizations can present more effective testimony, have the press give more respect to their public utterances, and otherwise exert more leverage as they seek to win on issues and obtain grants. There are many resources available for getting research assistance, including colleges, planning departments, and civic organizations.

Overall, the cases show again how neighborhood organizations are constantly called upon both to press on issues and to furnish services. Neighborhood people are simply not satisfied with an organization that seeks to avoid one of these functions.

SECO of Baltimore is probably the most successful at doing both. SECO has shown that a neighborhood organization can maintain a political stance and still retain grants from outside sources. SECO's position produces strains, but also many successes. SECO demonstrates the power that comes from representing a large territory and having considerable resources and members merged in a large coalition.

6. Case Studies III:
New Organizations Linked
to Politics and Government

In a democratic nation, politics and government are open to all who want to try to push their way inside. Gaining a slice of power is not easy, but it is usually possible.

Since citizens vote in polls close to their homes, neighborhoods have a special, important place in politics. Voting is organized by small pieces of neighborhood we call voting districts or precincts. Face-to-face campaigning in a voting district or precinct remains the one vote-getting technique more potent than television. It is not surprising that in a few areas residents have sought to use this political reality to improve their neighborhoods. They do this by building a neighborhood organization with an official or semi-official role in government or party politics.

We will look at three examples of this special kind of neighborhood organization. We will see that each has a structure made up of elected representatives from the voting districts, precincts, or other small subdivisions within the neighborhood. Beyond that, each has its own style of operating.

These cases represent a big switch. Most neighborhood organizations seek to stay away from direct involvement in government and party politics. The organizations we have looked at so far often seek to pressure governments and influence politicians, but usually they do not want to be tied to them. However, this is not so for the organizations in this chapter. They have chosen to be inside the political pot.

Advisory Neighborhood Commissions (Washington, D.C.)

The capital of the United States is a large city of seven hundred thousand residents. Although it is generally thought of as a place of monumental buildings, cherry blossoms, perpetual power, and sometimes corruption, it also is a city of neighborhoods. Most of the neighborhoods are populated by black, brown, and oriental people. Washington is a potpourri of minorities, with black people dominating its politics. Local government is shaped by a home rule charter enacted in 1974, with a special role given to neighborhoods.

Washington is one of at least thirty cities and counties providing a form of legal power for neighborhood organizations. It is an example of neighborhood organizations which are an actual part of government. Formal sanction for this comes from the 1974 city charter. In other cities with legally empowered neighborhood organizations the sanction might come from a city ordinance, state law, administrative order, or even a contract between local government and neighborhood organizations.

The legally empowered organization is a move toward neighborhood government and political decentralization. But it is only a small move. As Howard Hallman pointed out after studying Washington and other cities with legally empowered neighborhood organizations, "The relationship with local government is only advisory rather than delegation of decision-making authority or assignment of service operations."*

Washington's charter-sanctioned organizations are called advisory neighborhood commissions. They were first elected in 1975, from the thirty-six neighborhood areas into which city council divided the city, areas which did not always have the boundaries recognized by the already existing neighborhood organizations in the city.

Duties of a commission are to advise the mayor, council, and each executive agency and all independent agencies, boards, and commissions on any local government matters affecting the commission's area.

During their first year the new commissions in the District of Columbia struggled to establish procedures. One of the first questions to be faced was what role to allow citizens who were not commission

* Howard Hallman, *The Organization and Operation of Neighborhood Councils* (New York: Praeger, 1977), p. 4.

members who attended their meetings. Most commissions provided time on their agendas for citizens to speak. Some commissions asked whether participation should go beyond merely speaking.

For instance, in the DuPont Circle commission the question posed involved "full rights" for citizens. Residents on and off the commission proposed operating each meeting as a public assembly at which all citizens present would be allowed to vote, with the vote binding upon the commission. This issue was debated at length, with those in favor arguing for "maximum participation of all residents" at meetings, and others favoring "an orderly process" with only elected members of the commission having the power to vote. The latter position prevailed. The group agreed, however, to hold four open assemblies a year at which residents could take votes *advisory* to the *advisory* commission.

One of the chief arguments for "full rights" was that an advisory neighborhood commission needs strong citizen support if it is to have influence in city government. This was confirmed in the first year's activity of the DuPont Circle commission. Most of its meetings during the year were dominated by zoning issues. The commission made approximately twenty-five recommendations on zoning to the District of Columbia government, and about half of them were followed. Usually the commission's recommendations prevailed when there was active support for its position from voluntary neighborhood organizations in the DuPont community.

The basic District of Columbia law setting forth procedures, powers, and duties for a commission directs that issues and concerns contained in the recommendations of a commission "shall be given great weight during the deliberations by the [appropriate] governmental agency and those issues shall be discussed in the written rationale for the governmental decision taken." To date, each commission in the city has had a constant battle to obtain such consideration for its recommendations.

The somewhat affluent DuPont Circle neighborhood in northwest Washington contains about eighteen thousand people, a polyglot of black, white, and foreign. The neighborhood was divided by the D.C. city council into nine small districts, each containing roughly two thousand people. Each little district elects one member to the advisory neighborhood commission in a nonpartisan election. The nine members receive no pay. Most candidates run unopposed, and tend to be activists with experience in other organizations.

Under a charter provision, each commission receives a small cash allotment from the District of Columbia government, about $5,000 a year in the case of DuPont Circle. The amount varies for each commission area in accordance with population. Amounts are a bone of contention between commissions and the District central government, the commissions feeling that they receive only about half the funds called for by the charter.

With its funds, the DuPont Circle commission publishes a monthly newsletter, retains a half-time staff person, and gives small grants for community projects to other groups in DuPont Circle. Its meeting system has changed over time. It now holds meetings twice a month, with an open forum period at each meeting during which anyone may speak. Only the nine elected members vote, however. Most votes are unanimous.

The nine members of the commission elect officers, hold their meetings, hear residents, make decisions, and advise the D.C. central government. The commission's staff person handles mail and phone calls. Money is received and disbursements made. It operates like a small town council that has little power.

Since 1975, the principal goal developed by the DuPont Circle commission has been preservation of its traditional diverse residential character. It has sought to fend off a flood of commercial and condominium schemes for transforming various buildings and blocks. Preservation of a mixed residential character shapes the DuPont Circle commission's zoning recommendations, and lies behind the commission's successful support for designating the neighborhood a historic district. The commission has sought to have an unneeded public school recycled as a community center. Another issue given attention has been halfway houses for runaway youth, with many residents seeing the houses as a menace to the neighborhood. Others claim the halfway houses are essential for a humane and effective campaign to reduce vandalism, delinquency, and crime in the city and its neighborhoods.

Maintaining social fabric in affluent DuPont Circle is not easy. The neighborhood once had many folks of modest income who communicated as they sat on front stoops. But air conditioning and affluence eventually drew people inside, and now community organizations and newsletters seek to maintain communications.

The DuPont Circle commission has won many battles, and a major reason seems to be its working relationship with other neighborhood organizations within the area. The DuPont Circle commission has taken the lead in zoning cases. The neighborhood organizations have had primary responsibility for promoting historic preservation. Du-Pont Circle's status as a historic district means real estate developers must follow special regulations, which gives neighborhood organizations more opportunities to control change.

The DuPont Circle commission leadership is not pleased with the amount of recognition accorded it by the D.C. central government. Susan Meehan, who has been a commission member since 1975, says the D.C. government may or may not approach the commission in advance of making a decision about a plan or improvement for the DuPont Circle neighborhood. "We've even had a running battle to get proper notification on proposed zoning changes. It makes our work unnecessarily difficult. We may have to encourage some citizens to sue the D.C. government to get them to live up to the charter," declares Meehan.

In 1982 the DuPont Circle commission was seeking to rally support from commissions throughout the city to stop the D.C. council from imposing additional rules making it more difficult for the commissions to influence zoning change decisions. At the same time, recession was slowing conversion of DuPont Circle buildings to condominium use and bringing a return to rental housing, with the possibility of a resurgence of tenant associations. Such associations generally are allies and supporters of the commission. Unemployment was not a problem being brought to the commission.

Across Northwest Washington, in the more depressed, heavily black and Hispanic Adams-Morgan neighborhood, there is an advisory commission with a somewhat different history. The Adams-Morgan advisory neighborhood commission was controlled by AMO, the Adams-Morgan Organization, during its first few years of life, up to 1978. AMO, a long established neighborhood organization, ran candidates for the new commission in 1975 and elected nine of twelve members.

The Adams-Morgan advisory neighborhood commission is larger than the DuPont Circle commission because Adams-Morgan has twenty-five thousand people. It was a neighborhood of low- and moderate-income minorities in 1975 but has since been invaded by real estate developers and speculators who upgrade property, convert apartments to condominiums, create commercial space for chic restaurants and bars, and otherwise "gentrify" the neighborhood while pushing up housing prices and rents.

Both AMO and the local commission have sought to slow down this transformation and minimize displacement of long-term residents and small business people. AMO has been a rough-and-tumble organization prone to use a conflict approach, while the commission has been more polite and legalistic. AMO leadership feels that the commission has helped AMO attain more power.

The law requires that the appropriate advisory commission be notified before the D.C. central government makes a decision that would affect the commission's neighborhood. The commission is then to have a reasonable time to get its act together and make a recommendation. Adams-Morgan people have found this process especially useful in providing time to stir up opposition to a measure they fear will harm their neighborhood. In the early years of the commission, AMO and commission leaders planned and strategized carefully together as they sought to preserve and improve the character of Adams-Morgan.

Early on, the D.C. government interpreted the requirement on notification as applying only to legislation considered by council. Some of the advisory commissions claimed a wider interpretation, asserting that administrative decisions such as the granting of liquor licenses and demolition permits also should be subject to prior advice by the appropriate advisory commission. Their position was resisted by most central government officials. Some of the AMO leaders threatened to sue. Sensing a no-win situation, the mayor wrote an order to all city agencies requesting that they give notice to advisory commissions on important matters including licenses and permits. But the D.C. council keeps trying to restrict the commissions with new rules. Often the Adams-Morgan advisory neighborhood commission can find a consensus for opposing a change. But it finds agreement on a positive step such as building new low-income housing much more difficult to obtain.

The Adams-Morgan commission has stretched its efforts beyond city government. It teamed up with AMO to limit redlining in the neighborhood. When AMO filed a petition with the Federal Home Loan Bank against a local savings and loan association, charging it with discrimination against the neighborhood, the commission joined in formal negotiation on the side of the association. The result was an agreement protecting the neighborhood against redlining by providing an appeal process for anyone turned down for a loan. This achievement won respect for the advisory commission.

Issuance of liquor licenses has been a major interest of the commission. Both the character of a proposed operation and the impact on parking are of concern to the neighborhood. Through the advisory commission, some questionable liquor operations have been stopped. Frank Smith, long-time leader of both AMO and the advisory commission, believes "a good advisory commission should be at the point where an entrepreneur would come to it first to talk about his restaurant or liquor store, before applying for his permit."

Meeting monthly, the Adams-Morgan commission welcomes any citizen who wants to raise a relevant issue, or just attend to observe. Forty or fifty is considered a sizable turnout. Four times a year the commission promotes a town meeting to discuss the state of the community. These draw one hundred or more.

The Adams-Morgan commission receives about $9,000 per year, and feels it should get $18,000. The $9,000 is used for an office, secretary, telephone, and small grants to groups in the neighborhood to help along specific needed projects and services. It has published and distributed a guide to tenants' rights as part of its strong support for tenant associations.

For a while, the commission published a newsletter. Then it hit upon the scheme of buying space for its minutes every month in the *Rock Creek Monitor,* a local community newspaper. This disseminates detailed information about the commission to a wide audience, but does not provide the space to do all the things a newsletter can do.

When AMO elected most of its slate in 1975, established political leaders in the city were not happy about such organized effort. They saw the commissions and their new leaders as potential rivals.

Up to 1980, Frank Smith was the only advisory commission leader in the city who had been elected to higher political office (the school board). However, he remained optimistic about what the commissions could do politically. "They have the potential of forming real political machines," he feels. "In the future many of the city's political leaders will come out of the commissions." The Adams-Morgan commission, and four others in Washington's Ward 1, get together to discuss issues of mutual concern. Joint political action could flow from this. (Citywide joint action by all thirty-six commissions is forbidden by ordinance.) For the commissions to move from being advisory to having actual authority would require amending the charter, a process that would involve a petition and referendum.

Smith believes that many groups and people, besides the professional politicians, oppose the commissions. Says Smith, "Conservative people do not want the commissions to have more power. These people do not want change. The commissions represent potential change." There are also some neighborhood organizations in the city who see the commissions as rivals.

Since 1978, AMO's influence in its commission has declined. Some of the individuals involved have lost interest and dropped out. Attending both AMO and commission meetings was too great a burden. A few even chose to concentrate on the commission and dropped AMO. AMO membership on the commission declined from nine to four.

In 1982 the Adams-Morgan commission was dealing with trash, dog litter, and empty apartment buildings once intended for condo conversion. Some of its members were looking for ways to provide jobs for the neighborhood's army of unemployed but had come up with little beyond a plan to employ some youths in cleaning up trash. In Adams-Morgan unemployment is an old problem getting worse.

As AMO influence declined, the commission became more conservative, its membership made up of fewer minority members and more older whites. Smith seems to feel this situation will change when the need becomes great. "People have to come together around things they believe in. When the conservatives start blocking all the new low-income housing, then more liberal people will run for the commission. If they don't, then this could end up just another rich, white commission." Many in Washington feel the commissions from affluent neighborhoods seek little change and are satisfied with the influence they have.

"The commissions are here to stay," declares Smith. "They help the neighborhood movement solve two of its problems. They provide legitimate elected neighborhood representatives, and official neighborhood boundaries. They are helping many of the older civic groups by providing some funds, by giving awards, and by giving them support on critical issues."

"The more levels of government, the better," concludes Smith. "It keeps decision-making closer to the people."

Local government tensions stir beneath the surface in Washington. In most cities, like Chicago, they are much closer to the surface.

44th Ward Assembly (Chicago)

Chicago churns away, one of the world's great cities, given vitality by masses of minority people—black, Hispanic, Jewish, Slavic, Scandinavian, Appalachian, Italian, Irish, Asian—who struggle to hold what they've got and fight their way to something a bit better. For most people, the struggle revolves around jobs, politics, and neighborhoods. It is even felt in subway trains where bodies compete aggressively for space.

In the neighborhoods contention is old hat. Whites and blacks have tussled over turf for more than sixty years. Restrictive covenants were pushed by neighborhood improvement associations as early as the 1920s. Through the covenants, whites sought to keep blacks out of their neighborhoods. Saul Alinsky fashioned his mass-base, power strategy and confrontation tactics Back of The Yards in the 1930s.

Neighborhood renewal got its big start in Hyde Park—Kenwood in the 1950s, detonated by one of the first planning and change-oriented neighborhood organizations, the Hyde Park-Kenwood Community Conference. From its initiatives, and the belated power push of Hyde Park-Kenwood's leading institution, the University of Chicago, came the most expensive neighborhood renewal program ever carried out in the United States. It was a renewal effort replete with displacement (termed "Negro Removal" by renewal critics of the 1960s), but it built Chicago's first "stable interracial community of high standards."*

Hundreds of neighborhood organizations, varying in style, strategy, and coloration, have affected the city's life through the 1970s and into the 1980s. Much inventive organizing has been done as citizens and organizers have sought to deal with the city's volatile environment.

---

* For more about Hyde Park-Kenwood, see Julia Abrahamson's book, *A Neighborhood Finds Itself,* (New York: Harper, 1959). Julia Abrahamson was the first staff organizer of the Hyde Park-Kenwood Community Conference, a residents' organization begun in 1949.

The central reality for neighborhood organizations through the 1960s and most of the 1970s was Mayor Richard Daley, who dominated governmental, civic, and political life like a nineteenth-century corporate baron in a small town. His attitude toward neighborhood power was made clear during the time when antipoverty programs in many cities were generating opportunities for neighborhood people to make public decisions. The Chicago program, in contrast, was retained firmly in the hands of Daley staff appointees. When one of the authors asked the mayor about this in 1966, he stated: "Widespread participation would only bring conflict and bitterness, which Chicago has too much of already." He added: "It is a mistake for mayors to let go of control of their programs to private groups and individuals. Local government has responsibilities it should not give up."

One imaginative attempt of neighborhood people to move around the Daley barrier was the 44th Ward Assembly. Founded in the early 1970s, it was an unusual blend of governmental and citizen leadership. The assembly did much to improve life in its Lakeview neighborhood, and to some extent in all of Chicago by focusing on city legislation and public services.

Lakeview lies about five miles north of the Loop (Chicago's downtown). It is a dense neighborhood of two and a half square miles with over sixty thousand people. Judy Stevens, of the assembly staff, described the neighborhood as having "three vertical segments of population: the third close by Lake Michigan is primarily young Jewish professionals living in high-rise buildings; the central third has been largely Latino but is being moved out as young professionals buy and rehab the small apartment buildings in the area, and raise rents; the western third is primarily blue-collar working people living in two- and three-flat frame and greystone dwellings."

Public transportation is excellent. There are handy, bustling shopping streets and cool summer breezes near the lake. But there is too little park land, too few parking spaces, and too much traffic congestion. There is also a spreading nightmare of displacement, and growing thousands of unemployed.

The history of the 44th Ward Assembly revolved around a central figure, a professor/politician named Dick Simpson who was elected alderman (city council member) for the ward in 1971 with a promise to provide his constituents a more direct role in public decision-making. Simpson and his main supporters had worked in the 1968 McCarthy campaign, then founded the Independent Precinct Organization which involved activists from several wards in door-to-door politics, sometimes in open conflict with troops of Mayor Daley's regular Democratic organization.

The major purpose of the Simpson campaign of 1971 was to extend participation beyond the election process to the governmental process. Soon after his election, with advice and help from leaders of several church and neighborhood groups, Simpson moved formally to share his new powers with his political allies and other people of his ward. The instrument created to do this was the 44th Ward Assembly.

Members of the assembly were chosen in two ways. Open coffee meetings in nearly all the ward's sixty-four voting precincts each elected two delegates, and existing community organizations in the ward each selected a delegate. The first step in any precinct was for a staff member or volunteer to seek a host for a "coffee" at which the election could be held. The host contacted acquaintances in the precinct and invited them to attend, and flyers were distributed to others. The alderman or his representative attended each coffee and explained the assembly and the neighborhood problems it would address. After discussion, two delegates and an alternate were elected. A minimum of twenty-five residents of the precinct voting was considered essential for the election to be valid. If there were fewer than twenty-five, two delegates and an alternate were nominated and a petition was circulated in the precinct to obtain at least twenty-five signatures to confirm the election.

The first meeting of the assembly was held January 9, 1972. Sixty precincts were represented by 105 delegates, plus 55 delegates from community organizations such as church groups, block clubs, single-issue organizations, and the like, and 30 official observers who were public officials and representatives of organizations from outside Lakeview. The delegates ranged in age from fifteen to seventy-five. Several hundred citizens were also present as unofficial observers.

The assembly brought itself into being by adopting a charter (constitution) and approving a covenant between the delegates and Alderman Simpson. The covenant was the key to the assembly's gaining governmental authority. Simpson's new office gave him certain powers: a vote in Chicago's fifty-person council and a veto over major zoning changes in the ward exercised through senatorial courtesy (that is, the other forty-nine aldermen would support any individual alderman on a zoning question within the alderman's own ward).

Through the covenant, Alderman Simpson shared his power with the assembly. He pledged to be bound by the assembly on his votes in council and on major projects undertaken by his ward service office, provided the assembly adopted a position by at least a two-thirds vote. The assembly could initiate legislation, which the alderman would then introduce in council. It could establish priorities for the ward programs organized through the alderman's ward office. The members of the assembly also signed a covenant promising to participate actively in the assembly and to report back to the people of their precinct or community organization.

Simpson said he shared his power because of a strong belief in citizen participation in government. At the time of launching the assembly, he stated:

> At our meetings, I will try to convince the assembly members of my position. If I fail to do so, it is not important. It is wrong to assume the legislator always knows the correct answer. The only time I could refuse to vote with the assembly is if they were guilty of a clear infraction of the Bill of Rights.

Some observers of the political scene in Chicago viewed the assembly as Alderman Simpson's personal political organization, a mechanism for holding together his supporters, essential because he had no political party organization behind him. Many, however, believed the assembly served as a model of neighborhood participation in local government, its members debating and deciding important neighborhood issues. Supporters felt the assembly process increased civic knowledge and political skills among neighborhood people, and accomplished many things for the neighborhood.

The assembly established a load limit of five tons for the neighborhood's side streets. It picked sites for playlots and parks. It set policy on trash baskets and suggested changes in the city budget to improve public services. All of this was done with the assembly making decisions and the alderman and his staff carrying out the decisions. It proposed major legislation affecting all of Chicago, including an anti-redlining ordinance which, since being enacted, has been copied by other cities, and has influenced national legislation. It proposed amendments to a variety of city laws on unit pricing and condominium conversion that have been made part of the city code.

Important support for the legislative efforts of the assembly and alderman came from some of the neighborhood organizations represented in the assembly, and especially from mass-based organizations such as the Lake View Citizens Council, the largest and most important neighborhood organization in the 44th Ward.

The assembly formulated and proposed governmental solutions to neighborhood problems. The alderman carried the suggestions to city council and city departments. When his legislative proposals needed strong, visible support, this usually came from the Lake View Citizens Council. The assembly was an arena of debate and issue formulation inside government. The Citizen's Council was a mass pressure group outside government. Assembly members assisted the ward office with some of its service projects, such as telling residents how to comply with the city's animal control law and distributing information on tax reassessment of the ward. It did not operate social services. Strictly speaking, the assembly followed a mixed strategy, but the principal activity was of a political or pressure (quite low pressure) nature.

Assembly members annually distributed thirty thousand copies of the *44th Ward Almanac,* containing reports on conditions in the neighborhood and a guide to services, prepared by the alderman's ward office. They helped run the annual 44th Ward Fair, featuring local art, ethnic foods, displays by neighborhood organizations and institutions, entertainment by local performers, and children's games. The assembly undertook drives to raise funds for the local private food pantries which feed the hungry of the neighborhood. These activities helped build the neighborhood's social fabric.

Structure of the organization was not complicated. The base was the 150 or more representatives from precincts and from neighborhood organizations and institutions who attended assembly meetings and voted. (Any resident of the ward could attend meetings and speak, but not vote.) Annually, new assembly members were oriented to the work of the organization by the alderman at an introductory session. They were also furnished with a manual which explained what the assembly was, how it worked, and what it did.

Precinct delegates were elected annually. The turnover rate was high, running about 60 percent per year. This turnover disrupted the steady flow of communication. Some former delegates sat out a year or two, and then ran again.

The alderman chaired the assembly meetings. There were five standing committees. Most important was the steering committee, which had fourteen members besides the alderman. They were ten persons chosen by the assembly (six from precincts, four from organizations) and the chairpersons of the other committees. The steering committee arranged all assembly meetings and the open precinct meetings where delegates were elected.

Prior to each assembly meeting, delegates were sent an agenda listing issues to be discussed, and often background documents giving information on the issues. An emergency meeting of the assembly on a specific topic could be called by the alderman, or by 200 ward residents, by petition.

Individual delegates attended meetings, represented their precincts or organizations, debated, and voted. They reported back to their precincts or organizations, helped set up precinct elections, and implemented projects. They sometimes sent newsletters to the people they represented, held meetings, took polls, circulated questionnaires, and the like. Delegates could lose their seats by failing to attend three consecutive assembly meetings.

Delegates were bound by their covenant to report back to the people who elected them. Delegates from community organizations had little difficulty fulfilling this promise. They simply gave oral reports at meetings of their organizations, or wrote written reports for their organizational newsletters.

With precinct delegates, meeting the report-back responsibility was not so easy, for they had no ongoing mechanisms to utilize. Some distributed an occasional mimeographed newsletter, with mimeographing done by the alderman's ward office. In a rare instance, precinct delegates would call a meeting of precinct residents, especially around some crisis matter such as a large apartment building being changed from rental to condo.

However, two regular communications were sent each year to all residents. One was sent when precinct delegates distributed the *Ward Almanac.* The other was notification of the annual meeting in each precinct where delegates were elected. The local weekly newspaper, the *Booster,* which circulated by subscription to about 15 percent of the neighborhood households, carried full accounts of assembly meetings. Leadership of the assembly always felt more had to be done to improve feedback and interchange between delegates and the people they represented.

A major project of the assembly was the creation of a separate community zoning board, which held hearings on zoning questions and made recommendations to the alderman and city agencies. The alderman appointed the seven members of the board, with the approval of the assembly. The board was concerned with the physical future of the Lakeview neighborhood. Downtown zoning officials generally accepted the board's recommendations, and it succeeded in ending high-rise construction near the lake.

The assembly was a member of the National Association of Neighborhoods (NAN) because it believed in the need for a powerful national lobbying force acting on behalf of neighborhoods. Simpson was a leader of NAN from its beginning. In the fall of 1977, the assembly hosted a national conference of NAN in Chicago.

The assembly had staff assistance from the full-time aides in Simpson's ward service office. These were chosen after a wide public notification of openings, a screening of applicants, and interviews and final selection by the alderman. Simpson said he found his best staff among the people who had been active with him in political campaigns. Such staff generally stayed with his office three to five years and became able neighborhood professionals. They were trained on the job by the alderman.

Under Simpson, the ward service office had a budget of $60,000. The funds came from contributions ($8,000) and benefit affairs ($12,000), plus the staff allowances, expense allowances, travel allowance, and alderman's salary from the city, all contributed by the alderman ($40,000 plus). This budget covered the salaries for the staff working out of the ward office, rent, and other expenses.

Research for the background papers furnished to assembly delegates before meetings was organized by staff, and drew on various experts and sources in and out of the neighborhood. Greta Salem, working for a Ph.D. at the University of Maryland, studied the assembly and wrote a dissertation based on her observations which served as an evaluation of the organization. Beyond this, research activities related to the assembly were pragmatic and short-term.

Questionnaires were sent to delegates and member organizations from time to time asking for criticisms and suggestions. The ideas and gripes coming back were used by the steering committee to set agendas and to propose ways to strengthen the organization.

Each month the assembly followed a very focused agenda, concentrating on one or two important issues, problems, or projects. This brought new people to each meeting, and helped to build a reserve of people interested in running for delegate. Recruitment efforts of the organization revolved around the annual elections of delegates in the precincts. These elections constantly brought in fresh blood.

The main internal communication tool of the assembly was the monthly meeting announcement which went to several hundred, including delegates and alternates, neighborhood organizations and institutions, and others interested. It contains a detailed agenda for the meeting ahead and minutes of the previous meetings, and was accompanied by information on such issues as limiting high-rise construction in Lakeview, launching a sidewalk repair campaign, reducing vandalism, and regulating penny arcades.

The local newspaper announced meetings, and flyers were sometimes used when a particularly important issue was to be discussed. Lakeview is a large, densely populated neighborhood, with many apartment buildings. Informing all residents of the ward was a continuing difficulty for the organization.

Considering itself at least an informal part of government, the assembly sought a cooperative relationship with city officials from outside the ward. City department heads sometimes attended meetings, listened to suggestions, and gave help to the ward. At one of the first meetings of the assembly, the delegates told Simpson they did not want candidates introduced at their meetings. The assembly did not endorse candidates and seldom allowed them to speak as candidates, although they were allowed to attend meetings. Of course, many delegates were active in politics—but not openly at meetings of the assembly.

An important partner of the 44th Ward Assembly was Asamblea Abierta, a related organization which served as a vehicle through which Spanish-speaking people of the ward participated. It was formed in 1974 when Latino delegates found their participation in the 44th Ward Assembly hampered by difficulty with the English language. Meetings of the Asamblea were conducted in Spanish.

The Asamblea had little structure and a relaxed, loose way of operating. It had no officers, but did have a steering committee which planned agendas. People interested in an issue were free to pursue it. Issues tackled included rent gouging, and suits against the Chicago Transit Authority and the city of Chicago aimed at forcing them to hire more Latinos. It carried out its projects in close collaboration with the alderman and his staff.

The Asamblea also published a services directory in Spanish, helped some Latinos buy homes, and raised money for Latino agencies in the neighborhood. The service directory was financed by ad sales to local merchants.

Leaders of Asamblea Abierta felt it worked well without much structure because people interested in a specific project could plan it and run it without being bossed by entrenched officers. Also, it relieved volunteers of the temptation to spend time and energy on internal struggles.

Simpson did not run for reelection as alderman in 1979. As he voluntarily gave up the reins, he predicted the assembly would survive at least for a few years, that its participants would become more mixed ethnically, that it would turn to more joint effort with other Lakeview organizations, give more attention to crime in its local business districts, and perhaps create a new neighborhood planning commission to complement the neighborhood zoning board. At the time, aldermen in six other city wards had instituted some sort of citizens assembly, council, or zoning board to advise and assist them, or were planning to do so.

In 1979, new mayor Jane Byrne asked Simpson to advise her on how neighborhoods might be brought more directly into city government, and he helped her prepare a proposal for a citywide "Congress of Neighborhoods," which she failed to implement.

Simpson's successor as 44th Ward alderman was Bruce Young, a former president of the Lake View Citizens Council, who had been executive director of the neighborhood's Jane Addams Center of Hull House, a neighborhood agency in the settlement house tradition. He resigned from his Hull House job to become a full-time alderman. Throughout his campaign he had promised to continue the assembly.

When Simpson's term ended in the spring of 1979, the first assembly was out of business. Alderman Young spent the summer planning with staff, supporters, and other interested citizens to launch the new assembly in the fall. It meant new elections of delegates by community organizations and precincts. The basic structure and way of operating was to be continued. Some minor rule changes were considered, including one to raise above twenty-five the number of signatures required to elect precinct delegates by petition.

Important carryover issues to be tackled by the new assembly during the early 1980s included insurance redlining, control of condominium conversions, and establishment of a fair rent commission.

In 1980, Bruce Young suddenly announced his resignation as alderman, leaving the future of the assembly in doubt. Was the assembly such a well-established institution that any new alderman would have to keep it going? The answer came quickly. The machine elected its candidate and the assembly died—but its image as a useful model lives on.*

7th Ward Democratic Committee (Pittsburgh)

A neighborhood organization based on party politics is the 7th Ward Democratic Committee. It serves the same Pittsburgh neighborhood as the Shadyside Action Coalition described in chapter 5. The 7th Ward Committee is one of the thirty-four organizations in Shadyside which form the coalition.

The 7th Ward Committee is the official Democratic party committee for Shadyside, but it has long operated as an innovative neighborhood organization with considerable independence from the county party machine. It has sought to give the people of Shadyside more control over their own lives and territory by freeing them from outside machine control.

Its 1980s leadership and maverick ways go back to 1970, when a small group of independent Democrats organized a slate of candidates to challenge the neighborhood's old-time, entrenched party members. Battlegrounds were the thirteen voting districts of the 7th Ward. Two committee members (one man, one woman) are elected from each district, making a total of twenty-six committee members.

---

* The story of the 44th Ward Assembly during the Simpson years is told in full detail in a book called *Neighborhood Government in Chicago's 44th Ward,* edited by Dick Simpson, Judy Stevens, and Rick Kohnen, and available from Stipes Publishing Company, 10-12 Chester Street, Champaign, IL 61820.

The tradition-bound, entrenched committee members in power in 1970 were mainly concerned with getting and holding government jobs for themselves and their friends and relatives. Members of this old group faithfully followed orders from leaders of the county party machine. They had little or no interest in neighborhood matters.

The independent newcomers challenging the 1970 committee had been supporters of Senator Eugene McCarthy in the 1968 presidential primaries, and were participants in various neighborhood activities. In spirited door-to-door campaigns they won fourteen of the twenty-six seats in 1970, and elected new officers for the committee. It has been a different committee since that time. The committee is structured in a simple manner, with a chairperson, vice-chair, secretary, and treasurer. Small subcommittees are appointed from time to time to raise funds or research candidates.

In 1972 the committee joined with several other committees in the county to change the county party rules to provide that all committee members from each ward and suburb have a vote on candidate endorsements for public office at an annual party convention. This reduced the power of machine leadership and opened up the party considerably.

The new committee deemphasized "jobs-for-members" as an objective, and generally opposed the traditional patronage approach to government employment. This meant the new leadership gave up these historic patronage activities:

- constant pestering of elected officials to provide jobs for the ward committee and its friends
- endorsing job seekers on the basis of their party loyalty, rather than their skills and competency
- pressuring job holders in the ward to contribute time and funds to support the ward committee and its election campaigns

Turning away from these old-time patronage practices, the 7th Ward Committee adopted these new policies:

- if any person from the ward, regardless of party, asks for the committee's support in seeking a government job, the person will be interviewed as to ability to do the job; a preliminary background check will be made
- qualified persons will be supported for employment strictly on the basis of merit

- no pressure will be applied to any government employee to be active in politics or give any support of any kind to the committee.

This reshaped policy has served the committee well, assisting it to remain independent, and helping to advance the reform aims of a majority of its members. It enabled the committee to shift its attention from jobs to voter information and neighborhood issues.

Since being reorganized, the committee has done considerable political education, and it has used its influence to support the Shadyside Action Coalition on such issues as denying a state liquor license to an obnoxious night club, retaining the neighborhood's state liquor store, and enforcing zoning regulations.

The political year for the 7th Ward kicks off in January when potential candidates seeking endorsement for the spring primary parade before the committee, make their brief speeches (limit: 5 minutes), and try to answer tough questions tossed at them by committee members. These candidate sessions are held in church halls, open to all neighborhood people.

Committee members analyze the potential candidates, with each member deciding personally who to vote for in the endorsement convention of the county party. The convention is held in February or March, and committee members from the 7th Ward turn out en masse to cast their secret ballots. By turning out 90 percent or better, the committee exercises far more influence on endorsements than other committees, which often turn out 50 percent or less.

The endorsement convention names a party slate. The 7th Ward Committee believes that the party has responsibility to name a full slate of qualified primary candidates, but that once this is done each committee member should be free to choose who to support in the primary election. This freewheeling policy propels the committee into headlong conflict with party machine stalwarts in the county who believe all members of all committees should be bound to the endorsed candidates in a primary.

To give voters a chance to know something about all candidates in the primary election (there may be fifty to a hundred candidates on the party ballot, most of them little known), the 7th Ward Committee researches and publishes a voters guide which is delivered free to the neighborhood's five thousand Democratic voters.

Creation of each spring voters' guide is a spirited undertaking. A subcommittee sends a questionnaire to each candidate, reviews impressions left by candidates who appeared before the committee, and digs out information by other means. Amid arguments and debate the subcommittee drafts a short paragraph or two on each Democratic candidate in the primary and brings it to the full committee, which reviews it before determining a final statement. Much pulling and hauling goes on.

Statements about each candidate contain background data and an evaluative sentence or two: a candidate for judge "has been an outstanding addition to the court. Well-qualified." Another candidate for judge "has not demonstrated the outstanding legal ability that would merit election in this strong field of candidates." A candidate for county commissioner is "not a serious candidate." Another for county commissioner is "articulate but arrogant, able but abrasive." A candidate for city countil is "an unsuitable candidate with an unsavory background."

The voters' guide is eagerly awaited by voters and candidates alike, and raises a few hackles. It costs about $800 to produce, with the money raised at an annual spring spaghetti dinner, a major neighborhood social event with many elected officeholders attending.

In 1974, the city's voters approved a new reform city charter. Members of the committee helped launch the charter campaign. They persuaded able people from throughout the city to run for the nonpaying charter commission seats. Machine leaders in the city did not run for the commission because the seats paid no salary. A committee member became staff director of the charter commission, and committee members influenced the content of the charter and helped win votes for its approval.

After the charter's passage, the 7th Ward Democratic Committee took advantage of a charter provision to set up a beginning neighborhood government for the ward. The committee circulated petitions and won city council authorization for Shadyside voters to elect a community advisory board. Sworn in during 1980, the board has powers similar to Washington's advisory neighborhood commissions discussed earlier.

Once Pittsburgh's spring primary is over, the committee closes down for the summer but revives every September to canvass door to door to register new voters. Then committee members campaign for those Democratic nominees on the November ballot who are deemed worthwhile.

At the committee's regular meetings held every month, except for July and August, city and state legislators, the school board member, and the magistrate from the local area drop by to report and answer questions. Neighborhood issues are discussed and action decided. Most neighborhood issues are referred to the Shadyside Action Coalition, to which five committee members serve as delegates. Often a committee member becomes chairman of a coalition committee, and in 1982, the president of the coalition was a member of the 7th Ward Committee. Along with other organizations in the coalition, the 7th Ward Committee takes a large role in the coalition's annual convention.

Frequently the committee issues public statements on key political issues, and its fresh, critical stance sometimes wins space in the city's daily newspapers. An increasing number of independent-minded members of other ward committees in the city share 7th Ward views and struggle to modernize and transform their own committees.

Seventh Ward members have seen a few of their favorite candidates turn sour (that is, join up with the party machine regulars, favor economic interests over community interests, or just do a poor job) after winning elections. But enough winners do well to give the members hope. Many of the winners have shown skill and compassion as government officials.

There is also a 7th Ward Republican Committee. The two committees have had a friendly rivalry, and have cooperated in some efforts to register new voters. They work together at election time to ensure that each polling place is open on time with a full, qualified election board on hand.

When the Shadyside Action Coalition began, the Democratic committee persuaded the Republican committee to join. After a couple of years, the Republicans found the conflict distasteful and pulled out.

Fraternizing with Republicans raised few eyebrows, but when the 7th Ward Democratic Committee rejected street money it caused a stir, especially among the old downtown machine leadership. Ward committees in Pittsburgh have long been handed $40 or $50 or more per precinct by the downtown headquarters to aid and underwrite a large turnout of properly directed voters at each election. Traditionally the money has gone to "poll workers" who make sure their friends and relatives get out to vote.

Feeling the practice opens the way to corruption and vote-buying, and believing committed unpaid volunteers do a more effective job of getting out the vote, the committee in the early 1970s began to reject the downtown offers of street money. This further strengthened the committee's independence, and was another step in helping Shadyside people be masters of their own political turf.

A continual problem for the committee is turnover of members. Committee members move frequently, and new members have to be found. Young machine-oriented regulars often win election on the committee, hoping to help restore it to orthodoxy and thereby win points toward a machine-controlled government job.

The committee is frequently attacked by downtown machine leadership. In 1980 7th Ward Committee leadership affirmed its independent policy on candidates in a written memorandum, saying: "Each committee member is an elected party official, accountable to the voters of her or his district, and makes up her or his own mind on who to support in a primary." This memorandum fell into the hands of County Chairman Cyril Wecht, who immediately sent copies to all top county and city Democratic officials with a letter declaring: "I trust that all of you have enough personal pride, as well as interest and concern in the future of the Democratic Party, to keep this . . . 7th Ward philosophy in mind and begin to react and respond accordingly." Whether the response was to be bullets, bricks, a cold shoulder, nasty looks, or a ban on 7th Warders in government jobs was never made clear. Chariman Wecht's attack was reported in the daily newspapers. This won wide public support for the 7th Ward Committee, and helped make committee membership much sought after.

Although party rules limit the committee to two members per voting precinct, there are always some additional Shadyside residents who want to work with the committee. In 1980, the committee established the category "Friend of the Seventh Ward Democratic Committee." To become a "friend" it is only necessary to be a registered Democrat in the 7th Ward, be recommended by a committee member, and introduced at a committee meeting.

A "friend" has no voting rights but may attend and speak at any committee meeting or any meeting of a subcommittee. Friends receive advance notices and minutes of all meetings. They help the elected committee members register new voters, assist with organizing the annual fundraising event, research candidates for the voter's guide, and otherwise help make this neighborhood political organization effective. They are trained, ready replacements to fill in for committee members who move.

Several committee members and "friends" have gone on to serve in other important elected offices. A young lawyer is now the area's magistrate, and others have won election as state representative, city council member, delegate to a national convention, member of the community advisory board, and member of the state party committee.

A young independent Democrat from a nearby ward, long supported by the 7th Ward Committee, is now the city's neighborhood-oriented mayor. His battle against the machine in 1977 had strong support from members of the 7th Ward, some of whom held key positions in his campaign. A large chunk of his winning vote came from Shadyside.

Several committee members have been appointed to important, nonpaying advisory posts with the school district and in city and state government. Members have served as campaign managers for candidates for important offices.

Most members of the 7th Ward Democratic Committee place high value on competence, independence, openness, participation, integrity, and being well informed. These values reflect Shadyside, and are relevant to a strong neighborhood social fabric. Through its open meetings, door-to-door canvassing, and widely distributed voters' guide, the committee helps knit the neighborhood together. These activities communicate important values in a lively fashion, making them visible and meaningful to large numbers of neighborhood people.

Figure 3 compares independent and machine committees. Independents generally depend on motivations such as ego satisfaction, social contacts, the fun of controversy, fulfilling civic duty, and the chance to promote participation and improve public service. The softness of these incentives accelerates turnover. Machine members have hard motivation including the hope of jobs, money, and contracts. The difference in motivation seems to lead to a different outlook toward the voter. Eleanor Bergholz, who chaired the committee during 1980-81, contrasted independent and machine committee members: "Independents see the voter as someone to listen to and to induce into more active participation in community life. Machine people see the voter as someone to control and direct."

Figure 3

Comparison of Ward Committees
Independent vs. Machine

	NEW STYLE INDEPENDENT COMMITTEE	TRADITIONAL MACHINE COMMITTEE
Principal goal	Educate voters and encourage their informed involvement in elections; people of neighborhood control their own political turf	Get jobs for committee members and other party faithful in ward; produce votes for machine candidates
Role of chairman	Team leader facilitates committee members participating in decisions	Boss receives or makes all decisions; communicates them to committee members; signs off on government job applications
Meetings	Held at least monthly except summer; chairing of meetings sometimes rotated among committee members; two- to three-hour meetings, much debate and discussion	Held infrequently, two or three times a year; only chairman presides; brief meetings, little discussion, no debate
Issues	Take up many public issues of importance to ward	Limited to jobs, endorsements; shun public issues
Candidates	Interview prior to county endorsement convention; carefully evaluated	First meet at county endorsement convention; no attempt to evaluate
Information for voters	Publish frank voters' guide giving background information and evaluation on all primary candidates; get it to every household	Push machine-favored endorsed candidates by name; little information given voters

	NEW STYLE INDEPENDENT COMMITTEE	TRADITIONAL MACHINE COMMITTEE
Money	One affair a year to raise a few hundred dollars for voters' guide and take care of mailings; accept no street money from county committee for influencing voters on election day	One or more affairs a year, plus all in ward with a government job asked to make a substantial contribution; accept all street money
Voter registration	Systematic attempt to register all potential voters twice a year	Erratic; sometimes make an effort, often ignore
View toward party endorsements	Largely ignore, except in voters' guide mention all endorsements received by each candidate, including party endorsements	Absolutely sacred, follow 100 percent!
Non-committee members	Allowed formal affiliation as "friends" of committee; can join discussions at all meetings	Locked out, except at fundraisers

Strengths of independent committee: Promotes serious evaluation of candidates, openness and honesty in politics. Launches committee members into political positions of increased responsibility. Pays attention to neighborhood.

Weaknesses: Difficult to hold interest of all committee members over long haul. Tends to fragment party organization countywide.

Strengths of machine committee: Highly motivated members who maintain interest over long haul. Tends to promote cohesive party organization.

Weaknesses: Turns committee members into exploited robots, promotes irresponsibility, manipulates voters, entrenches elites. Tends to be anticitizenship and antidemocratic. Tends to center power downtown.

Comparison: The independent committee is bottom-up in its operation, while the machine committee is top-down. The former committee is neighborhood-oriented while the machine committee is downtown-oriented. A machine committee in the 1980s probably has difficulty reflecting the will of neighborhood people.

In 1982 machine forces regrouped in the 7th Ward and made a strong effort to recapture the committee. They ran seventeen candidates, needing twelve winners to assure themselves control. Independents organized a vigorous campaign, issuing a list of the committee's accomplishments during its twelve reborn years, with the declaration: "Now the committee is under attack by forces seeking centralized, political-plum oriented domination. Help thwart the attack on political independence in Shadyside." Through vigorous door-to-door campaigning, independents won all but seven of the contested seats and maintained firm control of the committee. They are likely to be in power for many years to come. The 7th Ward Democratic Committee provides a significant model for neighborhood politics.

Comment

Variety marks the three cases in this chapter. Each shows a distinct effort by residents to preserve and strengthen neighborhoods through organizing inside government and politics.

The three have achieved only limited gains. They are in a constant struggle for survival as independent organizations focused on neighborhood issues, and one has not survived.

In reality, these governmental-political organizations are add-ons, since their neighborhoods already have traditional organizations of the kinds discussed in chapters 4 and 5. The "add-on" organization can broaden a neighborhood's control over its own affairs and keep tabs on the city council members, state legislators, school board members, and other government politicos who are supposed to represent it. And such add-on organizations do seem to attract the interest and energy of neighborhood people not usually attracted to the more traditional neighborhood organization.

The 44th Ward Assembly and the 7th Ward Committee have both increased the power of neighborhood people by influencing officeholders and candidates for office. Perhaps a yet-to-be-created mixed neighborhood political organization could combine the techniques of both: a party committee with two or even more elected representatives from each voting precinct, plus representatives from every legitimate organization in the neighborhood. It could meet in assembly monthly to debate key issues and take positions; hear reports from city council members, legislators, and other key elected officials representing the neighborhood, and instruct them on needs of the neighborhood; and, before elections, hear and evaluate candidates for office, recommend the best to neighborhood voters, and campaign for them.

A question must be raised: Are governmental-political organizations worth the trouble? They soak up the time and energies of talented neighborhood people. With their relatively rigid organizational structures, they have a difficult time continually finding replacements for members who move or resign, since the new member must come from the same tiny district or precinct as the departing member. Especially questionable are the organizations which are an actual legal part of government, such as the advisory neighborhood commissions in Washington, D.C. Their powers are slight. Membership requires considerable time and there are no financial rewards. Few nonworking homemakers are around these days to take on such volunteer positions, as in the past.

Three researchers who took a close look at the Washington advisory commissions a few years back judged they had little influence on city government decisions. They found the commissions narrowly specialized in technical aspects of community development and physical planning, and concluded they had failed to develop active constituencies in their communities.*

Nelson Rosenbloom and Richard Rich have been studying similar government-linked organizations in Raleigh, St. Paul, and New York City. They find they offer important opportunities for participation to people in neighborhoods long without any organizations, although they confirm that neighborhoods with both a government-related commission and a cooperating long-time active voluntary neighborhood organization tend to have the most power.

Rosenbloom and Rich also find that the commissions tend so far to have inadequate powers and funds. They suggest that the commissions be given funds by city governments on a matching basis so that the commissions are motivated to go out and raise some funds on their own.

Another critical question raised about such elected neighborhood commissions is whether they are merely another layer of government removing citizens further from the real decision makers. This

* See Betty Woody, Ronald W. Walters, and Diane R. Brown, "Neighborhoods as a Power Factor," *Society,* May-June 1980, pp. 49-55.

question is related to the debate about whether commission members should act as elected representatives making their own decisions or as delegates carrying out the mandate of an open citizen assembly which makes the decisions. Those who favor an assembly argue that it is a vital mechanism which gives citizens a direct link to decisions, and breaks through one layer of government.

In cities where there is strong political party organization, it is possible that the seats on an elected commission would be captured by the party organization. Decisions then would likely be based on the needs of the party organization rather than on those of residents. This is less likely to happen when commission members are unpaid and have limited powers. Political party leaders often ignore unpaid offices.

It is possible to visualize an advisory commission which would become aggressive and attempt to stretch its powers. With support from the media, a hell-raising commission might have impact on city government. This happened at times in DuPont Circle and Adams-Morgan but could not be sustained over a long period.

In the future some neighborhood organizations may win an official role in government and take on broadened powers, with actual control over some matters. For instance, they might gain authority over zoning changes and developmental plans. This could mean residents' needs would be met more effectively, particularly in neighborhoods where an organization opens its decision-making to all residents.

The neighborhood organization with legal or semilegal status is still a fairly new element in the urban arena, and one that on paper seems capable of provoking far-reaching consequences. However, until these new organizations can generate constituencies and status, they are not going to have much power. They might even pass into oblivion if they do not produce more soon.

7. What Do We Learn from the Cases?

We have viewed neighborhood organizations at work in eleven U.S. cities. These experiences tell us many practical things about how to build a neighborhood organization. In this chapter we try to summarize and categorize these lessons. But first, we take a brief look at the big picture.

The cases confirm something fundamental about cities. Cities indeed do include in their polyglot makeup residential communities where human relationships evolve, relationships which are vital to the stability and creative thrust of cities. This is seen in the strong identification and recognition of neighborhoods found in the eleven cities. It is seen in the vigor of human ties and institutions. It is seen in the cadres of residents arising to defend their communities against threats.

Threats come from real estate investors, hospitals, banks, corporations, and the like. Sometimes these forces act directly, but often they act through government, which sometimes compounds the danger with schemes of its own. When neighborhood residents defend their community through a neighborhood organization, they seem able to ward off a threat, or at least to blunt its force.

In a democratic society, the members of a neighborhood community are capable of persuading government to become less partial to economic forces, or even to swing to the side of the neighborhood at times. But this happens only when the neighborhood organization is able to demonstrate that it can mobilize many people.

The well-being of cities probably depends on such collective action. Without it, injustices mount, needs go unnoticed and unmet, instability and decline eat away at the urban fabric. Cities then become unattractive for both people and businesses.

The cases indicate that mobilization by a single neighborhood organization is not sufficient to ward off all threats. Clusters of organizations are sometimes necessary to mobilize sufficient people and resources to handle the threats of large economic forces. Media attention also is necessary for mass mobilization.

The cases are not evidence that urban economic forces are evil and antineighborhood, but only that as hospitals, truckers, realtors, and the like pursue their legitimate interests they at times can harm the interests of neighborhood people and neighborhood institutions. Economic forces furnish jobs, goods, and services essential to cities. The need is for a balance between the power of economic forces and the power of neighborhoods. The cases show neighborhood organizations helping to provide this balance. Economic forces do not always get essential services to the urban people who need them most. The cases show neighborhood organizations working to fill this gap.

These cases were researched between 1977 and 1982, a time of decline in employment, productivity, and government funds. Have recession and the Reagan cutbacks affected neighborhood organizations? The cases indicate some impact, but it has been neither sudden nor devastating. Economic decline has been affecting most urban neighborhoods adversely for over a decade, and some much longer. Its pressures helped bring into being many of the neighborhood organizations in this guidebook.

Organizations such as the Barelas Neighborhood Improvement Association, Southeast Community Organization, and Upper Albany Community Organization long have had job creation as an objective. Youth unemployment particularly has been a concern of many of the organizations. The recession of the 1980s has been just another step down the ladder toward hard times. The size of the step has varied by sections of the country. Albuquerque and Greensboro seem to have come down little compared to Portland, Hartford, and McKees Rocks, Pa.

None of the fifteen organizations in the cases has been overwhelmed by economic decline. However, if the recession and cutbacks in government funds continue to become more severe into 1985 and beyond, then neighborhood organizations may be forced into drastic program changes. At that point, also, the big-budget organizations would likely face cuts in staff.

The authors find nothing in the cases to indicate that economic decline in cities will stop. In the final chapter a modest proposal is set out for involving neighborhood organizations and city governments in a new kind of effort to meet this decline.

The cases describe just fifteen of the ten thousand or more neighborhood organizations active in the United States. However, they do represent most types of organizations and give us useful guidance on how to organize a neighborhood. Some of the lessons from the cases arise out of successes and some out of failures, and some out of mundane experiences which never peaked as either successes or failures.

In this section we will seek to draw out of the cases specific ideas which might help guide us in building a neighborhood organization powerful enough to protect and improve a community. First we will review what the cases tell us about structure, strategy, and approach, and then go over specific skills in alphabetical order: administration; alliance-building; communicating; decision-making; evaluation; incentives; issues (their identification and selection); money-raising; planning, strategizing, problem-solving, negotiating; participation; power-building; recruiting; research; social fabric-building; staffing; training and leadership development.

Structure

As we have seen, most organizations start with a handful of enthusiastic people. Most are residents, although a few may be from businesses and institutions. Soon they recruit others to join them. Out of this usually comes an organization of individual members, as in Wichita and Albuquerque and most of the other cities, because this is the simplest and easiest structure. The members unite to get things done, with each having an equal vote. Each person's loyalty is directly to the new organization.

But we do have cases like the Shadyside Action Coalition and Southeast Community Organization, where the founders recruited block clubs, churches, and other existing organizations from the neighborhood to form a coalition. A coalition has instant strength derived from its member organizations. Eventually, over time, most coalitions tend to take in individual members.

In coalition organizations the leadership has to ride herd on the member groups or they will slip away. The first loyalty of member groups is not to the coalition, but to their own pressing concerns. In its heyday, the Shadyside Action Coalition rode herd by regularly obtaining commitments from member groups on how many people they would turn out for actions, and then checking to see how well they performed.

The coalition form has been useful in Baltimore, where the Southeast Community Organization covers many neighborhoods. Through a coalition structure each neighborhood and each neighborhood organization is able to maintain independent identity.

The Pittsburgh experience indicates that strong leadership can tend to turn a coalition into an organization of individual decision makers, and that this can be destructive to the coalition. Focus on Renewal in McKees Rocks further illustrates how coalitions tend to be dominated by a few strong leaders, in this case staff leaders.

Another potential weakness of the coalition form is that when even a small split occurs whole organizations drop out. We saw this happen in both Pittsburgh and Baltimore. But the coalition form still offers instant power and instant resources for people newly organizing a neighborhood.

In some of the cases we see organizations doing well with little structure. Especially, we saw this with the Arlington Park Neighborhood Association of Greensboro and the Western Addition Neighborhood Association in San Francisco. These two organizations accomplished some things as pressure groups without bothering about offices, staff, committees, treasuries, and the like. The Greensboro group did not even have regular officers. Their looseness allowed these organizations to concentrate time and energy on getting things done. However, internal affairs of the Arlington Park Association were not given much time. A strong, loyal constituency was not built. Resources were not gathered. When this militant organization was threatened by hostile government forces, it did not have the cohesion and support to survive intact.

The history of the older and more tightly organized groups has been that as soon as goals became complex, objectives less concrete, and the battles more difficult to win, these organizations feel it necessary to replace looseness with order and structure. In Wichita, for instance, we saw the Midtown Citizens Association, after years of success, move to seek a grant for a staff and office.

When an organization recruits both individual and organization members, as do the Shadyside Action Coalition and Focus on Renewal, there is opportunity to build more strength. This is a mixed strategy. Eventually disputes can arise over voting on important decisions. Organizations want more voting strength than the individual members. But how much more? Coalition organizations will always have some pressure on them to accept individuals.

The newest kind of neighborhood organization is one that takes an official or semi-official role in government or party politics. We saw three examples of this type in the case studies. As in most modern democratic governments, their members are elected by people voting from territories. Each tiny territory from which a member is elected is a subunit of the neighborhood. Such organizations are linked directly and formally to government or a political party. This structure shows potential, but so far organizations using it have been limited in power.

Figure 4 lists the four types of structure found in the cases, with direction on when to use each type, together with the strengths and weaknesses of each as revealed by the cases. Figure 5 sets forth the diverse committees created by the organizations in the cases. Most of the organizations seem to have about six to ten committees. Each neighborhood situation seems to require a different set of committees.

Strategy

Over time, neighborhood organizations swing back and forth between seeking what they want by pressure and furnishing services needed by residents. In the cases, most started with pressure, which is the low-cost strategy. Eventually they added services, when demands became strong and money became available. But they often seem to come back to a renewed use of pressure when new problems arise. Over time, too, most organizations move toward a mixed strategy. We see the mixed strategy in Albuquerque's Barelas neighborhood, in Baltimore's Southeast, and in McKees Rocks, where it was found to be fraught with risk.

We have seen a special breed of service organization, the Upper Albany Community Organization in Hartford, which seeks to concentrate on big-money economic development. We have seen some of the same desire in the Southeast Community Organization of

Figure 4

Alternative Structures for Neighborhood Organizations

TYPE	WHEN TO USE	STRENGTHS AND WEAKNESSES
Individual members	Fits most neighborhoods well when goals are simple and only a small amount of power is needed to get things done (Wichita and Albuquerque cases).	Simplest and easiest structure but can take a long time to build power and acquire resources.
Coalition of existing organizations	Useful when goals are complex and difficult, existing organizations and institutions are available and supportive, and immediate money and strength are needed. Especially useful in large area with several small neighborhoods (Pittsburgh [SAC] and Baltimore cases).	Instant power, but difficult to keep member organizations mobilized. Each has its own interest. Strong individual leaders can tend to displace organization members. When there is a split within membership, whole organizations are lost.
Mixed individual and organizational members	Can be built up when there is plenty of time to organize. Many organizations tend to go in this direction over time (Pittsburgh [SAC] case).	Can be difficult to allocate decision-making within the organization, since votes must be divided among individuals and member organizations.
Elected representatives from small geographic sections within neighborhood	Special structure for use when governmental powers or political party powers are to be exercised by neighborhood people (chapter 6).	Elections give organization claim to be truly representative of neighborhood. However, so far, power of such organizations mostly advisory.

Figure 5

Types of Committees

Program committees found within various neighborhood organizations:

Affirmative action	Planning
Community improvements	Public services
Community involvement	Recreation
Construction company	Retired skills project
Crime prevention	Schools
Development	Security
Downtown	Senior citizen
Education	Social action
Environment	Social services
Historical	Street beautification
Housing	Traffic
Land use	Transportation
Parks	Zoning

Housekeeping committees set up by some neighborhood organizations:

Entertainment	Newsletter
Finance and fundraising	Personnel
Membership	Socialization

Note: a typical neighborhood organization will have six to ten committees.

Baltimore. At times the leadership of both these organizations has dreamed of profits from their development enterprises, which would make their organizations financially independent of outside sources. But in over ten years they have never come close to realizing such profits.

The cases indicate that neighborhood organizations seldom make money through economic development.* There are small-scale operations like the supermarket in Southeast Baltimore which produced some funds for the neighborhood organization, but such instances are rare. By and large, neighborhood economic enterprises

---

* Even Chicago's The Woodlawn Organization, one of the nation's most famous neighborhood-based economic development organizations, has run into financial difficulties and had to be bailed out by the Ford Foundation.

are undercapitalized and ineptly managed, have fierce competition from private businesses, and cannot be counted on to produce money. Housing developments are the only proven enterprises in a number of neighborhoods. And even with neighborhood housing developments, there have been plenty of failures and heavy dependence on federal financial help, which is now declining and may disappear.

Figure 6 shows types of strategy, indicating when to use each, and their strengths and weaknesses. A description and discussion of the social fabric strategy will be found later in this chapter under the heading "Social Fabric-Building."

Figure 6

Alternative Strategies

Type	When to Use	Strengths and Weaknesses
Pressure	Organization has people but not money and wants to get government or a corporation to do something or stop doing something.	Simple way to start. Can make enemies. Difficult to sustain over long period.
Service	Pressing problems are affecting neighborhood; needs of people are going unmet; money and other help probably are available from outside sources.	Organization becomes dependent on outside funding source, but is able to offer a direct benefit to people.
Mixed	Mature organization operating expanded program with effective lines to outside sources.	Allows organization most tools, greatest impact; but any use of pressure can jeopardize funding.
Social fabric	Relationships and communications within neighborhood weak; want to build them up to have more stable community.	Concentrates on strengthening internal fabric rather than seeking external resources as other three strategies do.

Approach

Throughout the cases, organizations approach decision makers (targets) with a variety of intensities, depending usually on the difficulty of winning compliance. Many of the organizations, however, tend to use a particular approach.

Chicago's 44th Ward Assembly, the Salt Lake City organizations dominated by Mormon values, and Hartford's Upper Albany Community Organization emphasize cooperation and harmony. Wichita, San Francisco, and Portland utilized a campaign-negotiation approach in some of their efforts. In Washington's Adams-Morgan neighborhood we find militance and conflict, an approach relied on heavily also by the Shadyside Action Coalition in Pittsburgh and Focus on Renewal in McKees Rocks.

However, most of these organizations shift between hard and soft approaches as the occasion seems to demand. Figure 7 identifies when to use each approach.

Figure 7

Alternative Approaches to a Target

TYPE	WHEN TO USE	STRENGTHS AND WEAKNESSES
Cooperation	Decision maker (target) agrees and is willing to go along.	Keeps target as friend, but can be dull for organization members.
Campaign	Target needs some convincing; may agree on goal but not on how to reach it.	Costs are higher, but more interesting for members.
Conflict	Target does not agree on anything, not on goal, how to reach it, or even that issue exists.	Costs are very high; target may become permanent enemy; can be interesting and exciting for members of organization.

Note: Based in part on Roland L. Warren's article, "Types of Purposive Social Change at the Community Level," in his book, *Truth, Love, and Social Change* (Chicago: Rand McNally, 1971).

Specific Skills

Administration

The small-budget organizations pay little attention to administration. Not so the big-budget organizations. They have to pay attention, especially to financial management. Organizations such as Upper Albany Community Organization in Hartford and Southeast Community Organization in Baltimore hire professionals to keep records and oversee financial matters.

They have found that as they grow, other record-keeping becomes more complex and more important. The Hartford organization, for instance, found that having separate files kept by each department became a problem. It makes records hard to find. Storing records in a central file makes them much easier to locate. New, small organizations are probably well advised to establish central files from the beginning.

None of the organizations had staffs so large they were running into communications difficulties among staff members, but internal communication among members does require attention within most organizations, as will be noted in the communications section.

Board-staff conflict can disrupt an organization, as seen in the Hartford and San Francisco cases. This seems to occur where a strong staff director moves ahead independently without board knowledge and support.

Alliance-Building

In alliance-building, a neighborhood organization joins with other organizations to have more power for getting things done, but without losing its autonomy. This is sometimes called "coalition-building" and generally involves having allies outside the neighborhood, usually other neighborhood organizations. Alliance-building seems to be growing in most cities.

For instance, the Coalition for San Francisco Neighborhoods brings together thirty-seven separate organizations from various neighborhoods throughout San Francisco. These organizations have built an alliance which increases the influence of each organization when dealing with the mayor.

We saw that the Barelas Neighborhood Improvement Association and Western Addition Project Area Committee have not become members of the coalitions in their cities. This probably weakens both organizations. The Barelas organization is stable and eventually may find it needs allies and join the Coalition of Albuquerque Neighborhoods. The Western Addition organization belonged to national alliances, including the National Association of Neighborhoods and the National Association of Housing and Redevelopment Officials, but never felt at home with the small, voluntary groups which make up the San Francisco Coalition. Perhaps such support could have been a help in Western Addition's survival negotiation with the city's redevelopment authority.

Organizations like the Arlington Park Neighborhood Organization grow out of state and national networks. They have allies from the beginning. They refuse to form ongoing alliances with neighborhood organizations outside their networks. The result is that ACORN and Alinsky-formed neighborhood groups do not work closely with city-wide and national alliances other than their own. This probably weakens the neighborhood movement.

Some of the cases also point to the importance of a neighborhood organization maintaining friendly working relations with other organizations in the same neighborhood. We see this concerning the Southeast Community Organization. In San Francisco's Western Addition the neighborhood suffered because two organizations were at odds.

Alliances with corporations and other business organizations have occurred in Hartford and have potential in Portland. This may be a promising area for future development, but one fraught with difficulty because interests of residents and businesses are often different, if not in conflict.

Communicating

Clear and constant communications are vital to the operation of any neighborhood organization. The cases indicate that organizations spend much time and money on communicating, but are a long way from mastering the skill.

Most groups seem to rely on telephone calls, mail, and meetings for internal communicating among members. A few use newsletters, but most newsletters are aimed at reaching beyond members in a neighborhood. Telephone trees among members seem to break down easily. The cases indicate internal communications are not always given the attention they need, resulting in fewer strong relationships among members, and lessened participation and enthusiasm.

Considerable attention is given to communicating with the whole neighborhood. This wider getting out the word is seen as necessary to the survival and success of a neighborhood organization. Besides newsletters, these other mechanisms have proven useful: community bulletin boards, regular placing of articles in local neighborhood newspapers, buying space in a neighborhood newspaper, issuing an annual neighborhood almanac, publishing an annual voters' guide, public radio, and ethnic newspapers. Only one of the organizations described, in Portland, was using cable TV as a medium. This seems to hold promise. It takes study and care before it can be used well and requires a large investment of volunteers' time. Even when an organization creates effective TV programming, there remains the problem of attracting or building an audience.

In Chicago, the 44th Ward Assembly ran into difficulties because many of its elected precinct delegates had no regular gathering of constituents where they could report back and get direction on issues. Such a mechanism seems essential if a new politically oriented neighborhood organization is going to become influential and important.

Beyond the neighborhood, organizations need to transmit their message and make impact on the larger world from which they draw money, government services, and other resources. Besides the usual efforts to keep the media carefully informed about significant neighborhood matters, some other useful means are having a leader who is a celebrity and carrying out an occasional action that is dramatic and involves large numbers of people.

Media attention, as has been said often, amplifies the small voice of a neighborhood organization. This increases the organization's influence in dealing with large institutions, corporations, and governments. Communications can help an organization place its issue on a city's civic agenda, which is an important step in getting an issue resolved.

Decision-Making

Neighborhood groups, like democratic organizations everywhere, face the ancient difficulty of involving a maximum number of people in decision-making without becoming so bogged down in the process that decisions take forever. We saw this dilemma struggled with in the DuPont neighborhood of Washington. The issue is maximum efficiency versus maximum participation, and the solution is always a compromise.

Coalition organizations, including Shadyside Action Coalition and Southeast Community Organization, use an annual convention or congress to involve large numbers of people in major decision-making. There is a certain efficiency to this as much deciding can be done in one day. A convention generates heavy pressure to get the decisions wrapped up, and often is not so democratic as it appears on the surface.

The city of Portland's requirement is interesting, guaranteeing that residents can appeal a decision made by their neighborhood organization, or at least ensure their dissent is included when the organization makes a recommendation or request to city hall. The Hartford case illustrates how residents can revolt and insist on a share of decision power when an organization becomes elitist and loses touch with the people of its neighborhood.

Evaluation

Evaluation is an inexpensive way to improve the operation of any organization. But only a few organizations seem to use it consciously and regularly.

The Midtown Citizens Association takes an annual hard look at itself at an executive committee meeting. Barelas Neighborhood Improvement Association applies critical questions to every project at every meeting. The association has found this helpful to planning. Shadyside Action Coalition, in its militant days, made heavy use of evaluation—both for planning and for training inexperienced members. Sometimes it became brutally frank, subjecting a volunteer to embarrassment. The West Side Community Council in Salt Lake City went through annual goals meetings, required by its funding source, where the council's board measured strengths and weaknesses.

Organizations in Portland and San Francisco do informal evaluation.

Most of the organizations looked at do no regular evaluating, formal or informal. And none of the organizations utilize outside

evaluators to help see weaknesses and opportunities. Outside evaluation can often be arranged without cost, through colleges and universities, civic agencies, local governments, and the like.

Incentives

As this guidebook has emphasized, getting and keeping members
are basic tasks in building an organization. The key to getting and
keeping is incentive. People need a reason to join and stay. Discovering and offering the right incentives is a constant job for the
leadership of a neighborhood organization.

The 7th Ward Democratic Committee illustrates the difference
between hard incentives, such as jobs, and soft incentives, such as
ego satisfaction and social contacts. Obviously, hard incentives are
more powerful in attracting and holding members. Carolina Action
attempts to use merchandise discounts as a hard incentive. Shadyside
Action Coalition has offered unhappy and indignant residents the opportunity to put their anger to work. But it takes a lot of time to find
the angry people.

Southeast Community Organization, a coalition, came to the point
where it played hardball by requiring member organizations to be
active for the coalition if they wanted support from the coalition on
their issues.

The cases indicate that many organizations do not give serious attention to the need for incentives. This makes it tougher for them to
build strength.

Issues-Their Identification and Selection

The focus of this guidebook is process—how things are done.
But things are done for a purpose. The purpose of a neighborhood
organization is pursued through the specific issues it tackles: What
neighborhood defects does it try to correct? What threats does it attempt to blunt? What improvements does it aim to obtain? What services does it seek to furnish? Identification and selection of issues
are at the heart of an organization's work.

The purpose of Downtown Neighborhoods Association in Albuquerque is maintenance and improvement of the residential character
of its community. It pursues this by seeking to reopen its closed

school, chase out irresponsible absentee landlords, renew its main artery, and work on related issues. The organization regularly picks up new issues through its "gripe table."

Increasingly, neighborhood organizations try to stay clear of vague, nebulous issues. The Shadyside Action Coalition, particularly, has been conscious of the need to identify and select issues that are specific, concrete, and winnable. Southeast Community Organization found that committees which did not select clear-cut issues floundered. This is the organization which will not launch a new service unless that service is truly going to resolve important issues.

Local government and neighborhood groups in Portland have developed an elaborate system for identifying issues related to city services and capital improvements. Such a system probably can ensure that some needs are met before they become a serious issue.

The small cadre which leads every neighborhood organization has the task of making sure the issues chosen are relevant and feasible, as well as concrete. It is self-defeating to pick an issue an organization is not ready to handle. The more successful organization seems to be careful not to become involved in too many issues at one time.

Some organizations, including Northwest District Association and Shadyside Action Coalition, use research to help identify and understand issues. This will be looked at further in the section on research.

Money-Raising

Next to recruiting and training members, raising money seems to be the principal concern of most neighborhood organizations. There appear to be three approaches to money preferred by one or more of the organizations:

1. Get along on a small amount, so money-raising never becomes a problem.
2. Have a moderately sizable budget, but try to raise it without outside help.
3. Go big, but obtain funds from many different outside sources simultaneously.

Several organizations do find it easiest to have one large, outside source—but they go this route without preferring it. They would rather have several sources or a way to raise needed funds in their own neighborhood. Organizations which are or have been dependent on a single outside source include: West Side Community Council of Salt Lake City, dependent on the antipoverty program; Northwest District Association of Portland, dependent on city government; Western Addition Project Area Committee of San Francisco, dependent on the city's redevelopment authority; Advisory Neighborhood Commissions of Washington, D.C., dependent on city government; and 44th Ward Assembly of Chicago, dependent on the alderman of the ward. These organizations are the most vulnerable. If they lose their one source they will be staggered, if not killed, as did happen to one and was in the process of happening to a second.

The hardest organizations to kill off are those with modest budgets which raise their own funds from inside the neighborhood. These include organizations in Wichita, Albuquerque, Greensboro, and Pittsburgh. They get along without high-paid organizers. They may borrow organizers, hire them at modest prices, or have volunteer leaders do the job. But mostly the volunteers who make up the leadership cadre of the low-budget organizations serve as the organizers.

Some of the organizations have raised money in ingenious ways. In Chicago, a professor who was the alderman contributed his aldermanic salary. In Greensboro, member households gave $15 per year each. In Pittsburgh, neighborhood churches gave substantial amounts. Hartford corporations contributed heavily, and banks donated in Salt Lake City.

A few organizations have begun to investigate the possibility of selling an appropriate service or product, a high-risk operation.

Planning, Strategizing, Problem-Solving, Negotiating

The organizations that are successful seem to be continually in motion—planning, strategizing, problem-solving, and negotiating —as they work to resolve the most pressing issues in their neighborhoods.

As the cases reveal, the smaller organizations are mostly informal in the ways they carry out these activities which involve so much thinking, discussing, and acting. But even in these, the leadership cadres tend to be systematic and regular as they tackle issues. No organization in the cases has operated more informally than the Arlington Park Organization of Greensboro, but its movement from needs to pressure to solution followed a logical pattern.

Planning is intelligent thinking about the future. It generally involves information-gathering, which will be discussed under research, and the use of the information to map out rational steps toward action. Southeast Community Organization, a large organization, planned its new community development corporation through an elaborate, formal planning procedure.

Strategizing usually refers to the continual serious discussion that goes on among the members of the leadership cadre as they try to figure out how to execute their plans, meet their objectives, win their battles. It usually involves constant weighing, evaluating, moving forward, slipping back, switching tactics, revamping, struggling, and rejuvenating. The Adams-Morgan case in Washington gives us a sense of this process.

Problem-solving is viewed by the organizations in a couple of ways. It can mean all the steps from issue identification through research, planning, and evaluation with strategizing and negotiating along the route. Or it can merely be picking the right tactic and using it to get rid of an obstacle. The 7th Ward Democratic Committee was doing the former when it moved to make a new policy on the complex issue of patronage, but the latter when it fended off the attacks of an authoritarian county chairman simply by making sure his blasts were reported in the press. Upper Albany Community Organization encountered trouble with its constituents when it sought to concentrate on long-range projects at a time when its related block clubs and tenant associations wanted small, immediate issues dealt with.

Negotiating is the bargaining process that goes on when an active neighborhood group catches up with a target—the target being any person, institution, government, or other organization from which the neighborhood group would like to obtain something, such as a promise to take a certain action, or perhaps an agreement not to take an action. It is an orderly way of two parties dealing. An agreement usually comes only after some give and take on both sides. The Shadyside Action Coalition, in its early days, was a tough negotiator, generating pressure on targets which sometimes led the targets to feel they gained something big – getting the coalition off their back.

Participation

Participation is neighborhood people taking responsibility for their community by working seriously within their neighborhood organization. True participation means that people not only do the work of the organization but take part in making its decisions. The essence of participation is shared decision-making.

A constant source of conflict within neighborhoods and within organizations is who gets included in making decisions. We see this conflict in the DuPont Circle advisory neighborhood commission. Some people believed any citizen of the neighborhood should be able to join in deliberations of the commission and vote on decisions. They saw this as a way to widen participation and strengthen the community. But members of the commission could not accept this. They felt they had been elected to represent the neighborhood and that "orderly process" required they make the decisions. Their solution was to allow any citizen to speak at commission sessions, but not to vote. The 44th Ward Assembly followed the same procedure, which on the one hand is a limitation, but on the other hand makes a neighborhood organization a workable mechanism. In Focus on Renewal an effort was made to hold assemblies where all citizens voted, but in fact staff dominated.

Going back to Thomas Jefferson, some political philosophers have supported citizen participation as a practical means of education. They have seen it as a school of citizenship which imparts civic knowledge and skills. Certainly the members of the 44th Ward Assembly went through a rigorous and stimulating learning process when they decided on truck load limits for their streets and picked sites for playlots. The same can be said of members of the Midtown Citizens Association as they helped city government determine a swimming pool location. Such decisions require weighing of different interests, which is always an invigorating educational process.

A variety of organizations in one neighborhood gives people choice and increased opportunity for participation. This was obvious in the 44th Ward Assembly, where an Asamblea Abierta was developed to facilitate Latino participation. All of the new style organizations linked to politics and government, described in chapter 7, increase the opportunities for participation in neighborhoods where there are already voluntary groups, by providing an alternative kind of neighborhood organization.

Stability of volunteers can make it possible for citizens to take on greater responsibilities, simply because volunteers who stick around for a long time learn more skills, become more knowledgeable and competent. The Barelas Neighborhood Improvement Association particularly has benefited from long-term volunteers.

A citizen's right to dissent from a neighborhood organization decision is the objective of a requirement by the city government in Portland. The requirement applies to all organizations receiving aid from the city's Office of Neighborhood Associations. This should encourage participation by individuals. Residents who feel ignored, neglected, or left out of decisions can shake up a neighborhood organization, as we saw in the case of the Upper Albany Community Organization.

The use of special opportunities to stimulate participation was illustrated by the Western Addition Project Area Committee, which sought to turn its annual elections into exciting public events. The board members elected had considerable influence over decisions affecting the disposal of valuable land, which helped make the offices much sought after.

Power-Building

The organizations show an awareness of the importance of power—power being the ability to control people and events so that goals are achieved. The low-budget groups in chapter 4 seek power through people. They seek to be the voice of their neighborhood's citizens, occasionally showing their muscle at mass meetings, hearings, or conventions.

The media are utilized to amplify the organization voice, as with the Shadyside Action Coalition, but authentic support of large numbers of neighborhood people remains its basic source of power. Conventions are particularly appropriate to show the numbers really exist. An organization that has staff out front, with citizens not visible, does not realize its full power.

Money and property are a principal source of power for the big-budget organizations in chapter 5. Although their capital is limited, and they in no way can rival for-profit corporations, they do hope — through sponsoring shopping centers, housing developments, and manufacturing plants — to increase their influence as well as provide jobs and improve the conditions of their neighborhood. We see this particularly in the cases of Upper Albany Community Organization and Southeast Community Organization. However, in both these cases, the organizations have found at times they must still fall back on people as a source of power.

Sometimes ties to lenders bestow some power. We saw this in the cases of Salt Lake Neighborhood Housing Services and Downtown Neighborhoods Association.

Information is the third source of power, beyond people and money, but we see it utilized in only a few of the cases. An organization creates some of its own information as it makes plans, and this information gives it some influence and control, but most information for neighborhood organizations comes from research. The Northwest District Association has used basic needs surveys to give itself direction and bargaining power with city government. Downtown Neighborhoods Association has used information to try to influence school authorities. The Shadyside Action Coalition has made heavy use of research and found it not only can help influence government, but also assists the organization in strategizing. A well-researched presentation has more influence at a public hearing. The coalition has found serious and substantive information useful in obtaining attention from the media.

A combination of people power and money power is to be found in local politics. The Barelas Neighborhood Improvement Association recognizes this, and some of its leaders wear a political hat as well as a neighborhood organization hat, giving the association an indirect link to politics.

A direct link with politics and government was found in the three cases in chapter 6. The three organizations obtained power from their ties to the political system, but it is severely limited. The three organizations had constantly to push and fight to maintain their power and attempt to expand it a bit. There seems to be potential in such organizations, but it has not been realized yet.

As pointed out in the section on alliance-building, some neighborhood organizations gain additional power by being part of city, state, and national coalitions.

Recruiting

The ability to recruit members into a neighborhood organization is the most fundamental and essential of skills. Without this skill an organization will build little capability and will eventually die.

As we see with the Midtown Citizens Association, recruitment revolves around the leadership cadre. If stamped unimportant and shuffled off to those low in the ranks, it is not likely to happen. The leaders of an organization are most successful as recruiters when they approach people in a personal way, and offer them incentives. We see this process at work again and again in the cases.

The Midtown Citizens Association draws potential members to a pleasant potluck supper where the leadership shows there is a relationship between joining the organization and maintaining quiet, attractive streets. The small, friendly social event was also used in Chicago's 44th Ward.

Leadership of the Barelas Association applies personal one-to-one persuasion, especially upon people attracted by successful projects of the organization. The ACORN door-to-door style we observed in Greensboro probably works largely because of its personal nature. The same can be said for the quiet interview method of the Alinsky organizer seen in the case of the Shadyside Action Coalition. In its early years the coalition found people who were angry about an issue to be the easiest to recruit.

The Shadyside Coalition placed a heavy recruitment burden on its leaders, requiring them to bring in new volunteers in order to hold their position.

Specific incentives used include services. For instance, the Focus on Renewal organization uses its health and senior citizen services to attract members. Many organizations probably could do much more of this. Neighborhood Housing Services in Salt Lake City recruits members from among those who come to it for loans or to borrow tools.

Newsletters are used for recruitment, and the storefront office pulls in some people. The Southeast Community Organization used a massive, highly organized effort to recruit large numbers in a hurry. The 7th Ward Committee instituted a new class of membership to make possible enlargement of the organization.

Holding on to recruits will be discussed under training.

Research

Research is seeking out accurate information. It is searching that is done carefully and systematically. As pointed out earlier, it is essential to effective planning and strategizing, and often related to power-building. We saw particularly in the case of the Shadyside Action Coalition the great importance given to research. SAC felt that accurate information was essential to knowing about opposing forces. The coalition also used research as a way to train members.

We saw research skill used in Wichita, Albuquerque, and Portland. Some of the neighborhood groups persuaded other organizations to do research for them, as in Salt Lake City, where aid was obtained from city departments. In San Francisco, the Redevelopment Authority did research upon request.

Big-budget organizations like Southeast Community Organization take on complex projects and sometimes have their own staff specialists doing research. Focus on Renewal is a big-budget group but has no regular research program, its staff merely doing a little ad hoc quick study issue by issue.

Surveys of residents, examination of government records, and similar searching produce information especially helpful to organizations pursuing a pressure strategy. The information helps build pressure and helps direct it. It gives an organization more to argue about in negotiations, and enables it to make more accurate claims. Solid, dramatic information helps win attention from the press, as pointed out earlier.

However, as we have seen, some of the organizations in the cases make little or no use of research. They are missing a potent weapon.

Social Fabric-Building

The neighborhoods we have looked at are held together largely by their internal relationships. These relationships flow out of kinship ties, friendships, neighboring, shared values, local institutions such as shopping streets, churches, and drinking clubs, internal communications, shared history, and neighborhood organization. These neighborhood elements and the personal links they generate form the social fabric of the neighborhood.

The importance of social fabric to sense of community has long been noted by social scientists, but this knowledge has been little used to shape efforts for neighborhood preservation and improvement.

It may well be that when the social fabric of a neighborhood begins to break down, residents begin to move out in numbers beyond a normal, healthy rate, disinvestment occurs, and negative perceptions take over and influence the decisions of external and internal institutions and individuals. Attachment to the neighborhood probably declines.

Studies in Pittsburgh by Roger S. Ahlbrandt, Jr., suggest that original, purposive internal effort to strengthen the elements of social fabric could contribute substantially to solidifying neighborhood community. Ahlbrandt's studies indicate that people are less apt to move when social fabric is strong. Purposive social fabric-building perhaps would create a more stable environment within which development might more easily take place.

When a neighborhood organization concentrates on pressure or services, or a combination of them, the planning, committee work, decision-making, and implementation inevitably will generate some interaction among community people, businesses, organizations, and institutions, but this is incidental to its efforts. Social fabric is not the central focus. Attachment of people to the neighborhood is not the main concern.

A strategy which concentrated on building the internal strengths of a neighborhood probably would not need to ignore external opportunities, such as getting a state grant, or persuading city government to pave a street. A social fabric strategy might help a neighborhood achieve the cohesion and internal communications networks which would make it effective in dealing with outside targets.

In the Western Addition Project Area Committee case, the organizer described the need for people to get together. He illustrated a concrete program for building social fabric. The front stoops of DuPont Circle remind us of an element of social fabric from the past. In the future we can expect attempts by neighborhood organizations to use social fabric as a principal strategy for preserving and improving their neighborhoods.

Staffing

As a neighborhood organization grows and obtains a little money, it tends to hire paid staff. This seems to give the organization more continuity and stability. The leadership cadre may feel it takes a burden off their shoulders. We saw this trend at work in Portland and Baltimore, for example. And staff did seem to strengthen organizations in these cities. A standard staff set-up is to be found in Salt Lake City Neighborhood Housing Services, Inc.

But we also observed neighborhood organizations in Wichita and Albuquerque which achieved their objectives without staff. It can be done as long as there is a cadre of dedicated and skilled volunteers willing to give time to the organization.

The Shadyside Action Coalition was put together by an Alinsky organizer, so it had staff from the beginning. But in time it shifted from its own full-time staff to a purchase-of-staff arrangement which meant it had an organizer on call, spent less for staff, and had a wider variety of staff talent available. But it had no full-time staff of its own.

The leadership of the organization felt this arrangement forced them to do more on their own, and speeded up the development of volunteers. They feared a full-time staff organizer in time would give way to his or her own power drives and begin making decisions which should be made by the elected, volunteer leadership. A few leaders felt that when they did have an organizer available full time, citizens tended to bring their difficulties to the organizer rather than struggling to solve them themselves.

For a while, the unique feature of the Shadyside Coalition was the way it purchased staff from another organization. The coalition had control, since at any time it could drop the purchase arrangement and afford to hire its own full-time organizer. And eventually the coalition did drop the arrangement.

In voluntary neighborhood organizations each member supposedly has access to staff. This appears to happen more often where an organization hires its own full-time staff, and staff feel beholden to the whole membership. In the Shadyside Coalition purchase arrangement, the leaders were the only ones close to a staff which spent a limited time with the organization. Seemingly, ordinary members did not even know how to get in touch with such purchased staff. This contributed to a split within the organization.

Borrowing staff was more common than purchasing in the cases. We saw city government providing part-time staff services in Wichita, the alderman's office furnishing it in Chicago, and the antipoverty program lending it in Albuquerque. In Salt Lake City and

Portland, government furnishes full-time staff. In Greensboro, staff comes out of the citywide office of ACORN-affiliated Carolina Action, an office financed by the dues of members from throughout the city. The loose structure of neighborhood groups in Greensboro seems to place considerable control over such groups in the hands of staff. An interesting innovation suggested in Greensboro is the hiring of retired people as part-time staff.

In the big-budget organizations, staff play a large role and often are paid substantial salaries. In Baltimore high standards were set for organizers. They had to have skills as recruiters, trainers, researchers, and planners, and even have some knowledge of economics. They helped produce an effective organization.

In San Francisco's Western Addition there is a history of big staff budgets but difficulty in achieving objectives. In that city we see the pitfall of merely switching volunteers to the payroll. It doesn't always gain much.

In McKees Rocks, the staff ran the organization, and this probably held down its legitimacy and influence.

The role of the staff organizer will be discussed in much more detail in the next chapter.

Training and Leadership Development

Recruiting is the essential skill of getting members into the organization. Training and leadership development is the essential skill of helping them become useful to the organization, which is what usually holds members in the organization.

Only half the organizations looked at in the cases seem to have any serious concern for training. Of course, all of the organizations feel their members are being trained "on the job" and "by experience," that if they want training they can get it merely by "joining a committee." But neighborhood life is not so simple.

At least seven of the organizations described involve their members or staff in some kind of organized training. The 44th Ward Assembly had regular orientation sessions for new members. Midtown Citizens Association held informal orientation in members' homes for new recruits, and also took advantage of specialized training programs offered by the city for its more experienced members. The Shadyside Action Coalition in its Alinsky-oriented days was very training-conscious, holding regular sessions for members and even sending potential leaders off to the Alinsky training school in Chicago.

The Shadyside training sessions were open to all, and run by skilled professionals. In these sessions members learned how to check county courthouse records for the names of landowners, how to recruit people for actions, how to raise money, and a host of other useful skills. In addition to periodic training sessions for the general membership, there were special weekend sessions for clergy, and for the most active volunteers. These sessions offered in-depth training in strategizing, media handling, and the like. The coalition sought to develop a professional cadre of volunteers who might eventually eliminate the need for paid staff.

Northwest District Association in Portland also took advantage of training programs offered by city government. Big-budget Southeast Community Organization ran an intensive five-week course on community development and occasionally has sponsored weekend retreats and other short-term training.

The Western Addition Project Area Committee, in an unusual effort, tied training for all citizens to an all-day election. However, it had no money in its big budget for staff training. It did train its board members to enable them to understand the technical aspects of the urban renewal programs about which the board was making decisions. Focus on Renewal staff sought training at conferences put on by national organizations, and usually took some volunteer members along.

Training help is often available free from government, universities, civic organizations, and the like. But many organizations do not realize its importance in building the neighborhood organization.

8. Role and Secrets
of the Organizer

Behind any effectively organized neighborhood we will find one or more organizers. The organizer brings leadership and skills to the building of an organization. Without sustained pushing, cajoling, and building by the organizer, most neighborhood groups would lead short, toothless lives.

Janice Perlman, of the University of California at Berkeley, has studied neighborhood organizations across the United States. She has concluded that the organizer is the single most important factor in determining the success of neighborhood organizations.*

There are instances such as we have seen in Wichita and Albuquerque where local residents, as volunteers, have supplied the essential organizing skills. However, most strong neighborhood organizations eventually hire or borrow a paid organizer or two. Sometimes a neighborhood organization itself may raise funds to pay an organizer, but as we have seen the money usually is furnished by governments, foundations, and churches. Also, a settlement house, antipoverty agency, or university may loan an organizer from its own staff or student body.

Borrowing an organizer has strengths and weaknesses. The neighborhood organization does not select its own organizer, but usually must accept the person assigned to it by the lender agency. If the organizer borrowed is incompetent, the neighborhood group is go-

* See Janice Perlman's article in the book, *Citizen Participation in America,* edited by Stuart Langton (Boston: Tufts University, Lincoln Filene Center, 1978).

ing to be severely handicapped. A borrowed organizer generally will not concentrate completely on the affairs of the neighborhood organization.

However, there are strengths to the arrangement. The organization does not have to worry about a payroll or give a major portion of its energies to fundraising. Without a full-time organizer, the leadership is more dependent on its own thinking, deciding, and leading. This means more opportunity for volunteer leadership to develop.

A neighborhood organization is better off when it pays something toward the organizer's salary, even if only a token amount. This makes the organization a bit more independent.

The way an organizer goes about working will differ from neighborhood to neighborhood. The principal task of the organizer is to help people build an organization. Therefore, the organizer gives most time to recruiting and training members. Beyond these activities, the organizer exercises the many other skills discussed in the previous chapter.

The effective organizer helps people learn skills and gain a vision of a better neighborhood. The vision develops as people become aware of their rights to a safe and attractive community where there are churches and shopping streets, schools and medical services, and communications mechanisms. These and other institutions serve people's needs and help them build relationships which are the foundation of community.

Of course, paid organizers have their drawbacks. Sometimes volunteers slow down when a paid organizer comes on the scene. Organizers occasionally dominate and retard the development of members. Besides placing a large burden on the organization's finances, organizers often stay only a short time and thereby contribute to an organization's instability. But, as the Shadyside Action Coalition learned, the fires of action and success burned brightest when there was an organizer or two around.

An organizer may take one of three roles: enabler, advocate, or leader.

Enablers are the organizers with full faith in the ability of members to make sound decisions and take effective actions. Beyond recruiting and training, their role is limited to supplying knowledge, expertise, and resources. They participate in planning strategy and tactics but do not dominate or manipulate. Enablers are noncombatant trainers who help develop and equip the troops for battle, but stay out of the fight. They might help a neighborhood organization plan a march on an electric utility to demand lower rates for small users, but when the members march the enabler is a spectator.

The enabler organizer tends to be a detached expert, a neutral. Critics may call such an organizer "gutless." It is a relatively humble role. With organizations prone to strong action, organizers may have difficulty maintaining confidence if they are not putting themselves on the firing line.

The advocate approach has developed in reaction to the neutrality and "weakness" of the enabler. In the advocate approach, organizers become participants in the arena of social action. When their volunteer members meet with the mayor, they may do the talking. They are the civic "lawyers" arguing cases for citizen clients, as in the Focus on Renewal case study.

When the board of a neighborhood organization meets, the advocate takes a strong role in debate and decision-making. Sometimes the advocate gets out ahead of citizen partners, as when an advocate might speak out against an urban renewal plan which affected citizens had not yet considered.

The advocate role is a strong one, but often paternalistic, as such organizers seek to advocate what they believe to be "good" for a neighborhood. In an increasing number of relationships between organizers and members, neither the enabler nor the advocate role is wholly satisfactory. Members increasingly demand that paid organizers stand up and be counted, but not to the extent of taking over the policy-making role of members.

We now see organizers who are both advocates and enablers, yet are not completely either. These are the leader types. The residents with whom they work are partners rather than clients or constituents. Plans are jointly made. At a demonstration or public hearing the professional will be visible but not dominating.

A prototype of the leader organizer was Bob Connolly, who organized the Shadyside Action Coalition in Pittsburgh. He helped to develop a large cadre of resident activists. Together Connolly and residents set goals, planned strategy, and launched fights to close a night club, drive out a slum landlord, and get needed improvements from local government. The residents led demonstrations and spoke out at negotiation sessions. But Connolly was with them, helping plan the tactics and visible in their execution. When residents might falter or be intimidated, he was ready to act or speak to keep the pressure on. When he spoke it was clear he had the support of residents.

There is no one best single approach for every relationship. The white economic development organizer working in a black neighborhood probably is most effective as an enabler. The organizer pushing for improvement in treatment of the mentally ill might operate best as an advocate. In neighborhood organizations concerned with housing, renewal planning, or school reform, the leader role of co-responsibility seems to be called for. The sophisticated organizer carries a bag of tools that belong to all three roles.

A quality worth special mention is that of entrepreneurship. This means the organizer is an innovator and risk taker, one who creates or modifies structures, strategies, approaches, tactics, projects, and methods as necessary. Successes and failures of the entrepreneurial organizer are more spectacular than those of the routine organizer.

An entrepreneurial organizer has a zebra leading a march on city hall, helps plan sixty-minute meetings, and raises money and controls property by having his organization become the chief real estate broker in the neighborhood. Neighborhood organizations of the future probably will depend in large part on the skill of entrepreneurial neighborhood organizers.

Out of this discussion there emerges the image of an ideal neighborhood organizer: a person with conviction and values of his or her own that are strong, but not inflexible in the face of new knowledge and new experiences; who works with citizens for whom the organizer has respect, who is an educator continually bringing citizen partners new ideas, skills, and a sense of criticism; who is flexible in relations with resident partners, adapting as enabler, advocate, or leader in accord with the needs of a situation; and who does the same in taking a stance toward the object of change, always hopeful that being a cooperator will suffice, but ready to be a persuader or attacker as the occasion demands.

The ways an organizer goes about building an organization will differ from neighborhood to neighborhood. All organizers, volunteer or paid, accumulate knowledge of tactics, tricks, and ideas. These tactics and ideas tend to differ, and they become known as the "secrets" of organizers. They are viewpoints and methods and shortcuts for getting things done. The authors themselves are organizers and have built up small stores of secrets, some of which we are sharing here. In addition, some of the secrets of others passed on to us will be set down here.

The organizations which grow seem to be those which give attention to promoting participation. Public meetings where there is debate and decision-making on serious neighborhood issues will usually draw more people than meetings where there are merely speakers.

Organizers are agreed on the notion mentioned earlier that people are often recruited through self-interest. Some feel this is best approached through an issue that angers and frustrates, such as an ugly, empty boarded-up building in the block. Others say services that provide for real needs like children's dental care or job placement are the strongest magnet.

Organizations can also offer a concrete benefit tied to membership: members get a discount at a few local stores; members get to drink beer and socialize after meetings; members get low-cost home maintenance insurance. The whole incentive area is one all organizations need to study carefully.

Every neighborhood organization has two kinds of volunteers: those who have some smarts and experience and have been around awhile; and the greenhorns. The latter, the newcomers, should be given the "rat and trash" assignments, the basic work which is important but not earth-shaking. Here they gain experience and knowhow and get tested to see whether they really have a little fire in their bellies. To the brave go the fair, and to those who have demonstrated their competence and commitment should go the assignments of high responsibility. Their knowhow should not be wasted on routine phoning or minor committees.

One essential for retaining volunteers is that their expenses be paid. If they have assignments that cost sizable sums in phone bills, transportation, babysitting, and the like, volunteers, unless wealthy (which most aren't), will not be able to hold on without being reimbursed.

Many organizers find that the most responsive people in neighborhoods are the middle-income folks who own homes. These are the mass of Americans (about two-thirds of U.S. households own or are buying the home they are living in), and they are the greatest potential source of power in the United States.

Another note running through the secrets revealed by several organizers is "make it fun." If organization volunteers don't enjoy what they do, they won't be back. Meetings can be dreary. Plan them so they are not. Let there be some conflict, or a movie, but most of all keep meetings short, fast-paced, and focused on only one or two strong issues.

Many organizers feel that their primary business is building the organization, rather than initiating services or achieving reforms. They reason that a powerful organization can achieve whatever it chooses to do.

Door-to-door fundraising reaches the most people and trains the canvasser, who is a staff member and not a volunteer. It is known as a sure way to raise funds. A hard evening's work (4 P.M. till dark) will raise about $65 for the average canvasser. With 40 percent going to the canvasser as incentive, $39 per canvasser is left for the organization. Five canvassers would mean $195 per night. Operating five nights a week, this would mean $975 per week. Done forty weeks a year this would be $39,800, quite enough to provide a small staff, office, and postage for most neighborhood organizations. (As a matter of fact, all of these can be provided for a lot less, as little as $13,000.)

The canvassers are mostly young people. They need training, and they have to have nerve. It is a great experience for a beginning organizer, just as doorbell ringing is the best training for a successful politician. Givers are sent a monthly newsletter and so are brought within the organizational ring. This helps build the organization's constituency.

The neighborhood festival is a popular method which serves other purposes in addition to fundraising. It gives recognition to ethnic diversity, recruits and develops volunteers, and raises neighborhood awareness and pride. However, the only way to make big money at festivals is to have gambling. The consequences of gambling have to be weighed carefully.

A growing number of neighborhood organizations are casting greedy glances at the United Way. Here is a source of steady funds. However, traditional service organizations like the Boy Scouts and YMCA have had a death grip on most United Way money. It is difficult for a neighborhood group to become a recipient of United Way funds, especially if the organization engages in advocacy and militant action. United Ways are controlled by corporations and trade unions. The representatives of these established institutions give priority to highly visible, noncontroversial services.

A new way to enter the United Way system is through "donor option," which allows contributors to designate any nonprofit health or human service agency whether a United Way member agency or not. Many neighborhood organizations can qualify. By campaigning among residents in their neighborhood, and getting many to designate their neighborhood organization on their payroll deduction cards at work, neighborhood staff and volunteers can build a steady source of operating funds. Each hundred designations is worth $5,000 to a neighborhood organization. United Ways offer donor option plans reluctantly, but coalitions of neighborhood organizations can help make it happen.

For the future, contracts for services with local government may be an important source of money for many neighborhood organizations, as will be discussed in the next chapter.

For the organizer, visiting other cities to study what makes them tick, observing their neighborhood organizations, trading secrets with their organizers, is important. Such visiting freshens organizers.

Have more than one issue going at a time. This will involve more people, and if you lose one you can compensate by winning another. Hook up neighborhood issues with large citywide issues. It will get more publicity and support. For instance, if a neighborhood has a severe parking problem in one section, it might hook this to the need for a citywide residential parking plan. Also, it is useful (and fun) to hook an issue to some symbol. The redlining issue is hooked to an attractive young couple with five kids who can't get a mortgage. The expressway issue is hooked to a particularly handsome church which would be torn down. The zoning violation is hooked to a rich absentee landlord who lives in the suburbs.

During the past ten years, most organizers have come to believe that at least a small use of disruptive tactics is essential to an organization's getting results and respect. And some feel it is best to move in two disruptive directions at a time. For instance, while street demonstrations go on, a court suit is filed. The organizer moves people out of their old experiences to new ones where they learn new tactics and become comfortable with the new experiences, but apply them to enemies who are not familiar and so are put at a disadvantage in negotiations.

Always expect delay from established targets. They have been around a long time and anticipate they can outwit any new force.

The annual convention is a tactic made popular by the Alinsky organizers. It is a great show of strength and can have certain democratic features, although these are usually more show than reality, since many organizers have a way of staging conventions to ensure the "right" outcomes. The convention is an event that draws the press and gives participants a sense of excitement and power. It is a useful tool of recruitment, also. Generally the established elements of a metropolis such as government, banks, real estate developers, utilities, corporations, United Way, unions, and the like pay attention. It seems they do so especially if the convention is held in a prestigious downtown hotel. Such a location begets high visibility. At the annual convention officers are elected, priorities on issues set, resolutions passed, and the constitution and by-laws amended if necessary.

Here and there is an organizer with a negative view toward conventions. These feel conventions bring out too many diversified opinions and lead to chaos in an organization. The benefits of a convention are much smaller than the resources required to stage one, they feel.

Corporate and institutional people have one set of interests, neighborhood organizers and citizens have another set. They have to try to understand each other's objectives. The organizer has to understand the self-interest of the other side at all times, and play on that.

A Chicago organizer feels that the most powerful strategy is multigroup support on an issue: "Diverse groups such as the League of Women Voters, civic organizations, civil rights and militant groups, labor groups can hit from all sides, and can reach and affect all kinds of people with different outlooks," she says. Coalitions are important to the survival of neighborhood organizations.

A new difficulty is arising in neighborhood organization. The large territory of many neighborhood organizations has within it several small neighborhoods. These awaken to their identity. Ways have to be found to keep the small units feeling free and independent and yet part of the whole power base. The annual festival can help with this, as can a newspaper. Care has to be taken that government and other outside interests do not play one small neighborhood against another. We saw this problem dealt with in Baltimore through a multineighborhood coalition.

To attract and hold members it is useful not only to have clear objectives and be working on definite, relevant issues, but also to have a simple structure known to all, a well-publicized meeting place and time, and an ease of accessibility to committees and into decision-making.

If active members like one another, and are open to accepting new members, the organization is more likely to hang together during difficult days. When internal conflict arises, a period of intense activity on an important issue will help dissipate the conflict. If members share some basic values, and can have fun together, the organization probably will last.

A Portland organizer emphasizes that citizens and staff have complementary kinds of knowledge. In her view, paid organizers have the professional training to recognize symptoms and should have some ideas about alternative courses to resolve problems. Citizens, on the other hand, have the intimate familiarity with a neighborhood territory, resources, and social networks to supply staff with needed information, and to help decide which of several possible solutions might solve a particular problem.

A Pittsburgh organizer believes loose, informal groups can give more attention to issues as they are not wrapped up in the needs of their own structure. Loose, free organizations are more difficult for outside institutions to control and manipulate, and therefore such loose organizations can be freer and more independent, she believes. We saw this philosophy put to work in the ACORN group in Greensboro.

Some of the organizers who contributed to this chapter are: Paul Roden and Ed Schwartz (Philadelphia), Reno Aldrighetti (Montgomery County, Md.), Gerald Taylor (New York City), Jan Peterson (Brooklyn), Mary Lou Wolff (Chicago), Gil Rickets (Columbus, Ohio), Slim Coleman (Chicago), Donna Keck, Phil Perkins, Jon Lombardi (all of Baltimore), Bill Watson (Newark), Ellen Lurie and Dave Beckwith (Providence, R.I.), Paul Borrmaun (Milwaukee), Jack Kersey (Louisville), Dave Gustafson (Decatur, Ga.), and Lynn Dumond, Tom Murphy, and Ron Soncini (Pittsburgh).

9. The Future of Neighborhood Organizing: A Modest Proposal

Neighborhood organizing has had two major missions over the past two decades: organizing neighborhoods for advocacy and pressure and organizing neighborhoods for development and service. Each of these missions was originally exclusive. Advocacy organizers discouraged any funding from government agencies they were likely to attack in order to build independent local power. These advocacy organizers also renounced independent service initiatives in the community in order to keep external service agencies as targets of attack. They feared if they took on services they would be told that since neighborhood communities could furnish their own services, there was no need to confront government for them.

On the other hand, development and service organizers tried to build cooperative relationships with city hall and the federal government to obtain government resources for services, housing, and commercial revitalization in their communities. Grants and contracts for development, they believed, would be jeopardized by confrontation on community issues. Development organizers formed big-budget neighborhood development organizations that were distinct from the low-budget advocacy organizations.

Over time the walls between these two kinds of organizing have been breaking down, as we saw in the cases. Advocacy organizing has not always been able to resist the availability of government funds for community service and development. The Industrial Areas Foundation, organized by Saul Alinsky, and a bastion of advocacy organizing, is currently organizing a community development project in the Ocean Hill section of Brooklyn for the construction of five

178

thousand homes, using a combination of church, federal, and municipal funds.

The big-budget development organizations, on the other hand, have discovered that advocacy organizing at the block level increases the demand for services and development and gives them more clout. The development organizations can then represent themselves to local government as the logical suppliers for that demand. The Upper Albany Community Organization in Hartford, as we saw, assists block groups to demand improved community services, while it stands as the technical assistance facility in the neighborhood ready to accept contracts from city government to meet these needs.

More recently there has been some pulling back. As advocacy organizing has become compromised by development grants, community pressure has forced it back to a more independent posture, as we saw in Baltimore and Hartford. As development resources from government become scarce, those development organizations which had moved to use confrontation profitably now reduce that use. This tendency is visible in San Francisco. Trends in organizing will continue to change as conditions change.

What is the future of neighborhood organizing? What can it do to increase the power and quality of life of neighborhoods in a new era of scarcity and localism when the federal government is seeking to shove some of its responsibilities back to states and cities? To answer these questions, we must see the conditions under which neighborhood organizing began and how these conditions are changing.

A principal reason for the emergence of neighborhood organizations over the past thirty years has been the downtown renewal strategy of cities and the consequences flowing from that strategy. During the late 1950s, it was clear that massive suburban flight would follow on the heels of federal transportation and housing policy, as well as school integration. City governments, pushed by real estate developers, banks, daily newspapers, and other economic forces, decided to base their survival on downtown renewal and a land use policy that would allow the construction of highways to link downtown to the growing suburbs. A major part of government resources available for development of cities was invested in this strategy. As a consequence, neighborhoods were neglected with respect to both physical infrastructure and social services. Some neighborhoods were destroyed in whole or part by the urban renewal bulldozers or waves of dislocated people. Organizations emerged in many neighborhoods to fight the effects of renewal and demand an end to neglect. Some resources were retrieved in the form of improved government services and development contracts. The major push of downtown renewal continued, however, with just a few bones thrown to neighborhood advocacy and development.

The community revolt of the 1960s, with students, minorities, women, and others demanding recognition, spilled over to neighborhoods. Demands for participation and a share in urban power accelerated the growth of neighborhood organizations. The antipoverty program, begun in 1964, for a time provided rich opportunities and resources for participation, advocacy, and development, but the program quickly was reduced to impotency by politicians who feared the competition and by neighborhood antipoverty boards which squandered funds in patronage hiring, as we saw in San Francisco, or in poorly run, sometimes corrupt, service programs.

In assessing downtown renewal, it is probably fair to say that it preserved a large portion of downtown jobs which otherwise would have gone to the suburbs. And it helped city governments maintain a tax base. But it did leave a legacy of social disaster for the 1980s. As for the antipoverty program, it has limped on into the 1980s doing little to help even the victims of social disaster. For a time, some neighborhood organizations used its resources, as we saw in Albuquerque and Salt Lake City.

In most older American cities, a substantial population loss over the past decade has weakened social fabric and threatened tax revenues. We see viable and strong organizations in those solid inner-city neighborhoods where the remaining middle-class and working-class people — white, black, and Hispanic — live; and we see substantial territories of our cities with weak neighborhood organizations where a growing underclass of people is sinking into poverty, unemployability, mental illness, alcoholism, drug addiction, and crime.

The real question is whether our cities can remain livable. Can a renewed downtown and a few strong neighborhoods help a city maintain livability when a large underclass is a growing threat to its prosperity? The answer to this question lies in the limits of insecurity and blight that a general population can sustain. Can cities maintain quality of life if idleness and despair accelerate crime, promote civil unrest, and erode the tax base?

Present data show continued movement of middle-income people, including minorities, to the suburbs. It is problematic how many middle-class and working people the city can retain over the next two decades. Each upturn in the economy seems to produce more opportunities for working people to flee the city than it does unskilled jobs for the underclass.

As for the general transition of the economy, from an industrial to a high-technology base, many Sun Belt cities and suburbia probably will emerge viable and prosperous. The Sun Belt cities in the cases seem to be doing quite well for now, but even they contain the seeds of decline and an embryo underclass. The suburban working class will make it because they have the capital, personal networks, and educational motivation to pick their way through this vast change. This will happen for them in the normal course of private-sector investments and organization, with present levels of public support. Two-income, young professional couples restoring old urban houses will make it, although even these may leave if insecurity soars in the city. But masses of young people spawned by the underclass in cities will not be able to make this transition on their own. They will add social dynamite to the crowds of industrial workers whose skills are obsolete, the minorities who never had skills, and other unemployables. This volatile build-up casts a cloud over our urban future.

There is not sufficient incentive in the private sector to solve the motivation and skill defects of the growing underclass. Corporations will find all the highly skilled labor they can use coming out of community colleges and universities and settling in plants and offices throughout the Sun Belt, suburban America, and the downtowns served by rapid transit.

There is not enough political incentive, capability, or desire in the national government to solve this. This is a big country with world interests and vast power. It can withstand much waste of human lives and turbulence in its lower reaches without altering its aims and priorities. With shifts in population, the power of most cities in Congress is diminishing; and by tradition, our federal government has assisted, but not governed, the flow and direction of internal development. Federal resources will be required, to be sure, but the initiation and thrust for solution will have to come from elsewhere.

It seems probable that many cities cannot survive their growing poverty and pathology without a new kind of city-initiated economic development generated on a massive scale with a deep involvement of the private sector. In this era of localism, enhanced development for job creation will have to come from the initiatives of city governments energized and guided by community forces which give local government new attention, new commitment, and new force. Outside resources will be essential, but urban people are going to have to initiate a solution themselves, using city government, the only unifying, large-scale power instrument they have at their disposal.

In making this proposal, we are not extending present trends, or otherwise making a prediction of what will occur, but rather are proposing the kind of effort we feel must occur if most of our major cities are to remain human places where family life and neighborhood communities can grow and prosper.

A community-directed city government could have the incentive to confront poverty so that the city could survive as a livable place. The economic development efforts of such a city government would need to be massive, diverse, and creative—even unorthodox. Economic development would have to become the primary mission of city government and its allied neighborhood organizations.

City governments have gained some bits of experience with economic development in the past fifteen years, through economic opportunity programs, Model Cities, Comprehensive Employment and Training Act (CETA), and development departments which have sought to aid and encourage private businesses with tax abatements, Urban Development Action grants, infrastructure, below-market loans, and land acquisitions. But city governments have not seen economic development as their primary mission.

Cities do not fully comprehend this mission because, in fact, they do not have the power adequate for large-scale economic development. They do not have the capital and credit to do the job. But they are likely the only unit with the incentive to get the job started, even if their power, as traditionally understood, is inadequate for the task. It is proposed that city governments become engines of risk-taking and organizing, with a focus on enterprise, and bring in many outside forces. We are talking about all kinds of enterprise, large and small, profit and nonprofit, with neighborhood economic development only one part.

Political leaders in our cities are not ready for economic development as their principal focus, because citizens are not ready to accept this new mission. Citizens still think in terms of traditional services, and no mayor is going to cut his or her throat by failing to listen to the voters, most of whom are still removed from unemployment and oblivious of the underclass.

As the cases reveal, the threats of poverty, unemployment, federal cutbacks, and the unrest of growing masses of despairing people are still but specks on the horizon of cities—growing to be sure, but not yet disturbing most residents. The drifting Portland lumberjacks turning to crime to survive, Hispanic dropouts in Albuquerque without hope for decent jobs, rejected unemployed black youth in Hartford and Washington, and old people in McKees Rocks fearful the federal ax will take their life-sustaining health services are visible to discerning neighborhood organizations, however, and these signs can be a warning to act. This urban social decline calls for systems change.

Impetus for city government to shift to a new primary mission of economic development will have to come from the pressure of communal forces—neighborhood organizations, churches, issue groups, recreation clubs, racial and ethnic groups, labor unions groggy from recession, small businesses fearing bankruptcy, and similar forces which have their lives bound up in cities. Urban homeowners, whether working-class, middle-class, or the new two-income professional couples, now have substantial investments to protect—an incentive for taking action. It is proposed that neighborhood organizations begin to mobilize such pressure.

Once moving forcefully toward economic development, city governments will need to derive strength from their own national leagues and federations and to wheedle and leverage support from state and federal governments and the corporate sector. Big corporations can be cajoled and beat upon to cooperate, threatened with loss of congenial, efficient workplaces and sizable markets if they do not, rewarded with good will and more reliable employees and customers if they do.

For city governments to shift to a new primary mission of economic development, they will need to shed their old primary mission—now over one hundred years old—of service delivery. This mission of public works, social service, health, trash collection, police and fire protection, and similar traditional services can be farmed out, in large part, by contract to neighborhood organizations and private businesses. We have seen in the case studies neighborhood organizations competent and resourceful in service delivery. There are some dangerous functions, such as dealing with violent criminals, which would have to be retained by government, but neighborhood organizations and corporations could learn to handle most, often by hiring present city technicians.

City services are labor-intensive and can be made even more so by eliminating expensive equipment and creating more unskilled jobs essential to redeeming unemployed youth and moving them up and out of the underclass. Public service unions can be asked to cooperate to save the economic base of city government just as industrial unions have been cooperating to save the economic base of the auto and steel corporations for which they work.

With services shifted off its back, city government can move fully into economic development. City government cannot handle two major priorities at the same time. We suggest it spend 20 percent of its resources monitoring contracts to neighborhood organizations and private corporations, and 80 percent of its time and attention on economic development.

We suggest that this means mayors will be chosen, not on the basis of the potholes they fix, but because of the high-technology industry they initiate. Neighborhood organizations can handle the contracts to fix potholes. Citizens, in turn, can hold neighborhood organization staffs and boards accountable for the provision of adequate services. New mechanisms have been created for doing this which can avoid the waste and corruption of the antipoverty program. However, many issues of accountability are yet to be mastered. This matter would have to be given careful attention.

The question in all this for elected officeholders and neighborhood leaders is whether to risk a new approach for restoring the vitality of cities or let them be slowly overwhelmed by human misery. Will city government continue with its relatively passive role of services and facilitating development, or strike out in strong, active new directions to team up with communal forces and ensure that its people have training and productive work? This will probably call for new modes of neighborhood organizing, and new kinds of politicians.

We are not proposing an original departure. Great strides were made during the past decade to create federal and local mechanisms for supporting public/private economic development ventures in cities. Certain cities like Baltimore and Cincinnati made impressive gains and are withstanding the current economic slide a little better than most cities of the Frostbelt. But no city did more than scratch the surface of economic development. The federal government has weakened this evolutionary transition by curtailing federal supports and incentives. But as cities' economies worsen and crime increases, people are beginning to press their city governments to do something. The primary mission of all city governments by the twenty-first century may well have to become economic development.

This does not mean city government will own businesses, as some have advocated, but rather that city government will act as initiator, stimulator, organizer, leader, and lender of venture capital. It would use its power of eminent domain to provide sites, and its capital budget to provide infrastructure on a scale beyond anything yet seen. City government need not become the owner of any businesses established or expanded. It might, however, help many community-owned nonprofit corporations become owners of substantial enterprises.

This does not mean having a token city office of economic development staffed by a few good people. It means the reorganization of city government with professionals who can handle everything from organization and investment to recruitment, labor, training, motivation, transportation, planning, and other essential economic functions. We are talking about a highly qualified and professional city government that can work with businesses, numbers, and people on a vast scale.

Cities have been granting tax abatements to businesses, especially when new construction is involved. They have been providing streets and water lines and planning services to assist private corporations. They have assembled choice land sites for business expansion. But they have seldom tied such aid to jobs for city people. The jobs created often go to suburbanites or even out-of-staters. A city government focused on economic development would demand that a substantial percentage of the jobs created be set aside for city people, including apprentice slots for promising members of the underclass.

Cities would have closer ties with colleges, universities, and corporate research departments to midwife new high-tech small businesses and ensure they locate in some of the low-rent abandoned industrial buildings which dot inner cities.

Such a program would help turn the public schools into a job-oriented system with close ties to employers and incentives and motivational processes for what are now considered the dead-end children. Especially they would encourage, nurture, and give loving, tender care to small businesses with growth potential, including nonprofit and cooperative ventures begun by neighborhood people.

Under this mission the job of neighborhood organizing will be radically altered from its present state. Advocacy organizing will have to continue to build power so neighborhood people can keep a dominanat role in directing city government. It will have to agitate for more economic initiative by city government in consort with the private sector. Organizing will have to monitor politicians to keep them focused on the new task of development. It will have to help motivate the unemployed to learn new skills and to work as new opportunities unfold. It will have to promote the mentality of self-help so that neighborhood leaders accept the challenge of localism and welcome rather than oppose municipal contracts for service, which can both provide jobs for neighborhood people and also build interrelationships and thereby the fabric of the neighborhood.

On the development side, organizing will have to shape some neighborhood organizations into highly professional and skilled instrumentalities of service delivery so that they can meet the test of satisfactory service performance in their own community.

Within a new framework of economic initiatives by city government and service delivery by neighborhood organizations, advocacy and pressure for social justice and development for creative community will continue. Justice and creativity can only survive in a context of order and general prosperity.

A neighborhood organization is primarily a vehicle for the expression and actualization of every human being's responsibility to a community. The mutual sharing of responsibility to others by members of a neighborhood community, in the face of urban social decline, constitutes a system of common deliberation, purpose, decision, and power. These elements give neighborhood organizations a collective destiny and every individual, in the familiar vicinity of his or her life, the opportunity to lead a historical existence, to be part of a peoplehood going somewhere in pursuit of some definite purpose.

This proposal, we believe, keeps faith with this purpose.

Appendix:
Best Books on Neighborhood

The Modern Classics

Milton Kotler. *Neighborhood Government.* Bobbs-Merrill, 1969.
David Morris and Carl Hess. *Neighborhood Power.* Beacon, 1975.
Suzanne Keller. *The Urban Neighborhood.* Random House, 1968.
Jane Jacobs. *The Death and Life of Great American Cities.* Vintage, 1963.
Saul Alinsky. *Rules for Radicals.* Vintage, 1972.
Rachelle Warren and Donald Warren. *Neighborhood Organizers Handbook.* University of Notre Dame Press, 1977.
Roger Ahlbrandt and Paul Brophy. *Neighborhood Revitalization.* Lexington, 1975.
David O'Brien. *Neighborhood Organization and Interest Group Processes.* Princeton University Press, 1976.
Howard W. Hallman. *The Organization and Operation of Neighborhood Councils.* Praeger (hardcover), Civic Action Institute (paper), 1977.
National Commission on Neighborhoods. *People, Building Neighborhoods.* U.S. Government Printing Office, 1979.

Participating in the selection of these books were:

Roger Ahlbrandt	Neil Gilbert
Jerry Altman	Gerson Green
Seth Bargos	Patti Jacobsen
Geno C. Baroni	Bernie Jones
Robert Bish	Greta Smith Kotler
Bob Chandler	Peter Langer
Dick Cook	Judith Martin
Anthony Downs	Elinor Ostrom

Joseph Parko

Janice Perlman

Bernard H. Ross

Jack Rothman

Henry J. Schmandt

Derek Shearer

Dick Simpson

Kitty Smith

Raymond J. Sturyk

Donald I. Warren

Esther Wattenberg

Zan White

Frank Woolover

The preceding books are the modern classics about neighborhood, chosen by knowledgeable people and listed in accordance with number of votes received. The following are a few of the recent neighborhood books selected with the aid of the *Journal of Community Action* and listed alphabetically by author.

Recommended Recent Books

Roger S. Ahlbrandt, Jr., and James V. Cunningham. *A New Public Policy for Neighborhood Preservation*. Praeger, 1979.

Philip L. Clay. *Neighborhood Revitalization: Issues, Trends and Strategies*. National Endowment for the Arts, 1978.

Anthony Downs. *Neighborhoods and Urban Development*. The Brookings Institution, 1981.

Robert Fisher and Peter Romanofsky, Eds. *Community Organization for Urban Social Change—A Historical Perspective*. Greenwood Press, 1981.

Rolf Goetze. *Understanding Neighborhood Change*. Ballinger Press, 1979.

Jeffrey R. Henig. *Neighborhood Mobilization—Redevelopment and Response*. Rutgers University Press, 1982.

Joan E. Lancourt. *Confront or Concede: The Alinsky Citizen-Action Organizations*. D.C. Heath, 1979.

Ed Marciniak. *Reversing Urban Decline*. National Center for Urban Ethnic Affairs, 1981.

Arthur J. Naparstek, David E. Biegel, and Herzl R. Spiro. *Neighborhood Networks for Humane Mental Health Care*. Plenum Press, 1982.

Sandra Perlman Schoenberg and Patricia L. Rosenbaum. *Neighborhoods That Work: Sources for Viability in the Inner City*. Rutgers University Press, 1980.

Donald I. Warren. *Helping Networks: How People Cope with Problems in the Urban Community*. University of Notre Dame Press, 1981.

About the Authors

JAMES V. CUNNINGHAM has been a neighborhood organizer in Chicago and Pittsburgh, and is now Professor of Social Work at the University of Pittsburgh. He is the author of *The Resurgent Neighborhood, Urban Leadership in the Sixties,* and *A New Public Policy for Neighborhood Preservation* (with Roger S. Ahlbrandt, Jr.).

MILTON KOTLER was the founder of the National Association of Neighborhoods, and is now vice-president of the Center for Responsive Governance, Washington, D.C., and managing editor of the *Journal* for *of Community Action.* He is the author of *Neighborhood Government.*

Index